T0128886

The Plane Truth

Keith Goodrum

iUniverse, Inc.
New York   Bloomington

The Plane Truth

iUniverse books may be ordered through booksellers or by contacting:

iUniverse
1663 Liberty Drive
Bloomington, IN 47403
www.iuniverse.com
1-800-Authors (1-800-288-4677)

*Because of the dynamic nature of the Internet, any Web addresses or links
contained in this book may have changed since publication and may no longer be
valid. The views expressed in this work are solely those of the author and do not
necessarily reflect the views of the publisher, and the publisher hereby disclaims
any responsibility for them.*

ISBN: 978-1-4401-1143-3 (sc)
ISBN: 978-1-4401-1144-0 (e)

Printed in the United States of America

iUniverse rev. date:3/20/2009

ADEN 1963-1965

Chapter One

I learned of my prospective posting to the Middle East, while I was stationed at a Joint Warfare Establishment in the West of England, at a very quick interview with my Commanding Officer, quick, because he had mislaid my overseas posting document, much to his embarrassment, which had laid underneath all the other miscellaneous files which congested his 'In' tray and made for total administrative disarray and in consequence, his forgetfulness had made for a tardy notification to me, of a very important event in my service life. I should have had six weeks notice of this posting, according to Air Ministry doctrine and because of a lapse of diligence, by my superior, which was not unusual in this multi-force type of operation, it was cut, to two weeks.

In that fourteen days I had to arrange all of my family affairs and get fitted out with my Khaki Drill (KD) uniforms ready for the journey to the British Protectorate of Aden, which was geographically situated, at the extreme south tip of the Republic of South Yemen, surrounded on the east by the Indian Ocean and on the west, by the Red Sea and to the north by the desert and the Jebel Radfan mountain range.

It was my misfortune to draw Aden as a posting, when there were so many other wonderful exotic places in the world where one could potentially go as a servant of the Queen. However, my hapless situation, of necessity, had

1

to be dealt with on an adult footing, so I resolved to do all that was required, in the time allowed, to put all my affairs in order and duly present myself at the appointed place of departure, on the appointed day.

My wife and two children would have to remain in the United kingdom, until such time as I could be given official Royal Air Force married quarters, which would only come if I were to be classified as a 'Key Person' for the operation to which I would be assigned. Some personnel, 'Key' or not, would not uproot their families and take them abroad, the reasons for which were two-fold, firstly it was a major move and schooling and family ties precluded it, secondly, it was a war zone and the idea of putting their loved ones in any kind of jeopardy, seemed foolhardy. I however, resolved to bring my family to my place of duty at the earliest possible time.

The two weeks went by very quickly, prior to my departure and having said a tearful good-bye to my family, I proceeded to the designated Air Force station, by bus and train, and duly arrived that evening for my induction to the transit operation in readiness for the flight the following day, to the Middle East.

Flight trooping operations were contracted out to commercial airlines and the following morning the assembled contingent of Army, Navy and Air Force personnel, proceeded to London Gatwick Airport for transportation to the appointed destination, Aden. It was December seventh 1963, a date, which is, indelibly, imprinted in my memory and as we took to the air, I had a sense of foreboding, as my country faded into the distance, so I made myself as comfortable as possible, if the term comfortable, can be applied to a troop configured aircraft seating arrangement. Eight hours and we would be in the hot humid land of the Arabian peninsular. Thoughts of the unknown, were provoking and tended to heighten the imagination, which was in no way conducive to a restful flight, so I turned my mind to my family and friends at home in England.

Chapter Two

Arriving in Aden, at the Royal Air Force Station of Khormaksar, was quite a unique experience and stepping off the aircraft into a very hot humid atmosphere, was akin to walking into a very hot kitchen and the air seemed to blast over my face and precipitate an intake of air into my lungs, which made me feel very uncomfortable.

Looking around at the scenery, I could make out the shape of the rock formation of the only mountain in the Protectorate, which I was later to learn, was named Sham Sham, which to this day I have never known its meaning and I was reminded of the song and well known military march "The Barren Rocks Of Aden'. This was a country of dry desert and scrub land, the only comfort being the seas which surrounded the peninsular, which was a comfort to many of us in the coming months, for the bathing was refreshing, however dangerous, from the multitude of lurking sea creatures and did bring a sort of relaxation, to an otherwise, claustrophobic existence.

As we approached the baggage claim area of the civil aviation terminal, there were several uniformed, heavily armed police and army personnel, which seemed very much out of place, as our flight had no dignitaries, nor apparently any cargo that would require such a show of protective force. As I collected my personal belongings from the baggage area, I mulled over what situation may cause such a show of strength on a normally well-guarded

Airfield. I was later to learn the reason for the armed militia, which would, in many ways, set the scene for the next two years.

Terrorism was rife in the middle east, as there was much dissension in the Arab world concerning the demarcation of the Arabian Peninsular and the fact that the British Protectorate of Aden and protected states in the area, did not find political satisfaction in the bordering Arab states, which stretched from the then, twin capitals of the Yemen (Sana and Taiz) through to the Egyptian capital, Cairo, where all the terrorist activities in the United Arab Republics were coordinated and from where all propaganda emanated, orchestrated by one Colonel Gamal Abdul Nasser, the President incumbent.

All insurgencies were aimed at the British military forces and political personnel, residing in the areas, where the loyalist Arab factions required the protection from those who would seek to subvert the democratically elected governments.

On this particular day, coincident with my arrival in the Protectorate, the Governor General, who enjoyed a political appointment for an indefinite period as described by the British Foreign Secretary, was due to leave Aden for an official tour of the territories for which he was responsible, duly arrived at the Civil Airport Terminal which was situated at the western end of the Khormaksar airfield, which was the only civil airport in Aden.

As the story was recounted to me, it was a few minutes before noon, when the Governor General was ushered through the doors, which led to the Dakota, DC3 or C-47 aircraft, as it was known in military circles, waiting on the very hot, concrete, hard standing, approximately twenty yards from the building. As his aids walked with him to the aircraft there was a furor in the terminal, caused by some local Arab workers, which at the time was not indicative of any imminent danger to the boarding party. It was however, subsequently learned, that it was one of several decoy moves, to deploy the security police and armed military personnel to a false location, allowing those who would terrorize, murder and destroy, to perpetrate their dastardly deeds.

A minute later, there was a thunderous explosion, as the Dakota was hit by a bazooka shell, fired somewhere from the causeway, which connected the Aden Protectorate to the desert by way of a local Arab community of Ash Shaykh Uthman, situated at the far end of the causeway, approximately five miles from the airfield, where a breach of the carefully planned defenses might occur, a single figure appeared from somewhere behind the air terminal, dressed in the traditional Arab garb of loose flowing robes, turban and leather sandals. This individual raced towards the Governor General's party, all of whom were attempting to retreat to the relative safety of the terminal, brandishing something in his right hand, which was later identified as a grenade, his obvious intent to launch it at the fleeing group, hoping to kill or maim the Governor General and or his aids. At a point where he was about to throw the grenade, the would- be assassin, was struck by a bullet fired by one of the bodyguards in the group, which precipitated a fortuitous situation for the Governor General's party, but a sad, very messy, fatal situation for the dissident, as he fell on the primed grenade and was dispatched into oblivion in a trice.

Success or failure of any attempted assassination, must of necessity be a highly organized fine-tuned, disciplined operation, especially when the intended victim is a high profile dignitary, with bodyguards and coordinated security measures to counteract such incursions is imperative. This very amateur effort to kill and maim a prominent official, was indicative of those who were behind the whole dissident operation, but of necessity, these malicious attempts to disrupt the regimen of law and order in a democratic society required protective, practical policies in order to mitigate such activities.

Typical of the terrorist activities, the hit and run philosophy, did not in any way make for effective results, but did ensure a highly trained internal security system to be implemented and maintained at a considerable cost to the host nation, both in monetary units and personal effort expended, to ensure a relatively safe environment, in which to live and work.

To say that the dissident Arab factions, were aggrieved at the loyalist, separatist Arab communities, was to understate the situation. It was an all out war from the inception of these pseudo-western capitalist societies, however democratic, brought about by the hateful, vengeful, procommunist Governments of a United Arab Republic, the formation and prime purpose of which, had been lost in the bitter enmity of trying to impose their will on the elements of society who wished to be self-governed under the banner of democracy.

To engage an enemy in an area as geographically wide and deep in terms of square miles, as is Saudi Arabia, ultimately becomes a task of such enormity, that the logistics of warfare, in an area where mountains and deserts divide friend and foe by thousands of miles, overshadows all strategies of actual physical combat, and detracts and negates the ideology for the original instigation of the act. Furthermore, to engage an enemy, which was vastly superior in warfare technology, in open conflict, would be total folly, thus, it was easier for the dissident elements to perform their cowardly acts of terrorism and not confront head-on, the forces of the loyalist factions.

Sana and Taiz, are joint Capitals of the Yemen and all propaganda was channeled through the public airwaves of both radio stations, initiated by Cairo radio and was, of course transmitted to the Protectorate of Aden, where it was received with incredulity, as nothing of the context of the verbiage was accurate and the local Arab and British populous of the Aden townships were somewhat bemused and totally in unison condemning the derivation of such fabrications.

The main thrust of most of the propaganda was engendered by the Government of factions that embraced the Democratic processes of Government. Gamal Abdul Nasser's hatred of the Jews and most European countries was well known and documented in perpetuity. His daily Broadcasts to the Arab nations consisted mainly of decrying the British Forces for committing such atrocities against the Arab nations, all of which were fabrication, however, it succeeded in agitating the masses, who, unwittingly accepted all the lies and deceptions in the name of their Islamic religion. After all, how could a leader of the stature of the Egyptian President, lie, to his followers, he was a devout Muslim and could not be party to any such scurrilous activity.

Directing tirades to the uneducated, uninformed elements of the Arab communities in Saudi Arabia and the Yemen, did not in many cases, have the desired effect, as certain factions, who were more worldly and informed and who considered the economic and social welfare of the Arab people, to be of paramount importance, than following a punitive doctrine, in which there could be no winner.

Chapter Three

Having survived the most recent, but not the only attempt on his life, the Governor General, who was a British Knight of the Realm and a very skilled diplomat, decided to make a concerted effort to gather all the current information on the insurgencies and terrorist activities and produce a document which would be presented to the British Parliament, in a vain effort to inculcate some urgency into the ranks of the Bureaucracy, hoping to precipitate an early political settlement with the dissident elements, through formal negotiations between all warring factions.

To enable a comprehensive dossier to be prepared, The Governor General gathered together, all the military and civil leaders operating within the Protectorate and requested ideas and strategic options for the current situation pertinent to the South Yemen incursions, the outcome of which was extremely enlightening and provided potential resolutions for the cessation of hostilities.

Attending the meeting were the senior members of the British Army, Royal Navy and Royal Air Force, the Commander in Chief being the Naval Admiral. Representing the Federal Regular Army, which was a loyalist Arab militia, was the senior officer, who was a colonel with a distinguished campaign record in desert warfare and a very respected commander. The Prime Minister and his deputy of the local Federal Government were in attendance, both of whom, were accomplished political figures in the Arab community. All concurred, that stringent measures were required to bring about a peaceful solution to the existing conflict, and the Governor General was adamant in his resolve, to point out the foibles of the present political strategy, which the incumbent Socialist Party of Great Britain, so arrogantly decreed, from their remote corridors of power, some four thousand miles away.

The whole thrust of the Governor General's paper to the House of Commons, laid out the existing situation, which was known to all those who had lived it for several years, and was supposedly known by the British Prime Minister and his Cabinet, as they were updated on a daily basis, by both military and civilian factions, stressing the importance of a political settlement, as there was no possible chance of a military solution due to the vast territory needed to be occupied and protected at any given time.

His communiqué was dispatched to the United Kingdom two days after the meeting and it was expected that there would be a reply within two weeks, as it was a matter for the Foreign Secretary and the Joint Chiefs of Staff to meet and formulate a plan which would be presented to the British Prime Minister, who would table a motion for the House of Commons to vote on, after a full scale debate and much partisan bickering, the result of which would be a mandate for the continuance of the status quo or some other intricate plan, which would of necessity, require a protracted period of time to initiate and negotiate. Whatever the outcome, the present situation would maintain for another few months.

History had created the mode and method by which the all disputes within the Arab world were settled and to say that the situation had improved over the last two hundred years would be overstating the situation.

When the idea of democratic reform in the guise of duly elected representatives of the people arrived, concurrent with the colonial annexation and modern world doctrines, the ideology was not altogether embraced by the various tribes and races indigenous to the vast desert lands of Arabia and it engendered a more animus reaction, to that which was expected by the more contemporary leaders of the time, some of whom were educated and ultimately indoctrinated in the western scholastic idiom, either in Great Britain or the United States of America.

It was not difficult to prognosticate the reaction of those who still lived isolated lives, borne out of thousand of years of tradition, as opposed to the relatively few, who were coddled the modern day western style of life. It was a situation, which would not be resolved in a matter of months, nor years, it required a generation or two to affect a completely new ideology, which would be accepted by all in the United Arab Republics.

The British Protectorate of Aden was classified as a war zone for the period of time that the colonial effort afforded a token military force to give the democratic processes time to evolve and establish a system of government, more in concert with western capitalist philosophies, which in itself was an optimistic project, given the fact that the Protectorate was a very small isolated strip of land, surrounded by the might of the Arab world, constantly bombarded by extraneous propaganda, which was an unsettling influence for the common people, who regarded themselves as Arabs and for all practical purposes identified with their neighbors who embraced the same Muslim religion.

Aden, had a very small indigenous military force, namely the Federal Regular Army (FRA), which comprised a very well disciplined and organized force, composed of local loyalist Arabs, trained by the British Army, in all the basic requirements of small arms and a limited amount of anti-personnel weaponry.

Supplementing the infantry was the Camel Corps, consisting of a highly trained body of men, whose prime function was to operate in the more remote desert areas, where the camels were in their element and a totally efficient source of transport.

In the more relaxed periods, especially on public holidays, the camels competed in races, similar to those held in the United Kingdom, where horses are the prime mounts. In all, the FRA, probably numbered around one thousand men, which, on a military scale, compared with other Arab nations, was Lilliputian

The British Army, Royal Air Force and sporadically the Royal Navy were the Peace-keepers and the only means of protecting Aden from the dissident insurgencies, which would mainly come from the desert to the north. However the port of Steamer Point also had to be guarded, as it was the one shipping port accessible to the Red Sea and Indian Ocean, where supplies would be imported from the world at large, thus it was a target for sabotage and required a military vigil at all times.

To put the whole scenario in perspective and to allow some scale with which to gauge the adversarial picture, the dissident factor should have a collective value, as all the individual skirmishes were not coordinated as a concerted war effort, in fact the bands of warriors were from tribes living in the mountains in villages so remote from each other, that at no time did they ever meet, nor in fact, know of the others existence. It was the couriers from the insurgents headquarters, in Taizz and Sana, with orders from Cairo and other political agitators, that created the segmented actions in sporadic and inconsistent time periods. As previously stated, the terrain was so vast and hostile to any would-be incursion, that any form of offensive or defensive action, was entirely random in nature. Hence, as history has recorded, the outcome of such a conflict, was a permanent stale-mate.

The Villages in the Mountains and valleys of the Jebel Radfan, were purely agrarian and self reliant, as they were isolated in the main and inaccessible to most commercial entities, thus, most of the western comforts of life were unavailable to the population and the quality of living spartan, to say the least.

Some literary pundits would consider the environment as biblical. The men of these villages were weather beaten, hardened mountain men, whose fighting prowess was borne out of defending their properties and chattels against marauding tribesmen from diverse areas of the local mountains, their arms consisting of ancient muzzle loading rifles and very sharp bladed curved swords and scimitars. These tribal encounters were of long standing origin, which indeed, could have had roots in ancient historic times. Little did the tribesmen know that they were fighting other tribesmen, who were controlled by the Cairo syndrome in the grand scheme of things to vanquish the British Army. Divide and conquer would be an apt maxim, were it not the antithesis, of the original concept. Guerilla warfare properly coordinated in areas where the enemy has a disadvantage, because of unfamiliar terrain, can be pernicious to say the least.

With the natural traits of warriors and the time with which to find other ways to expend their energies, the crops having been planted and their animals well tended by the women of the village, they were ideal candidates for any subversive element who might want to use their talents to carry out some basic forms of subterfuge, for scant reward, such as the laying of mines and the setting of ambushes on the more frequented dirt roads, leading into the mountainous regions. It was thus, that the insurgencies became realities and a bane of the military forces trying to counter such villainous activities in such a vast, uncharted area of rugged terrain.

Chapter Four

The British Army Garrison in Aden consisted of several Infantry, Armored and Parachute regiments, all of whom were specialized fighting forces, their tour of duty being approximately one year, during which time they would carry out a variety of duties.

Internal Security duty consisted of armed patrols in the domestic living areas, airfields and beaches where any form of terrorist activity, would disrupt the whole stability of the Protectorate, hence it was a duty which was not favored by the armed forces, as they were easy targets in the close confines of homes and buildings, which could be used to hide a potential threat which was a constant cause for concern, hence the infantry regiments took their turn performing the Internal Security operations.

External operations, consisted of a tour of duty in the forward areas of conflict, which could be either in the mountains where continuous sniper and minor skirmishes occurred daily, or in the approach road areas where mines were planted to disrupt the flow of traffic to the forward positions and in many cases caused heavy causalities to the allied forces and to uninformed, unsuspecting Arab travelers, using the roads for camel and donkey trains, carrying a variety of wares for sale in the remote villages of the Radfan Mountains. It is a sad testament to the perpetrators of such terrorism that a bomb knows no ethnicity nor can it differentiate between male, female, child or animal, however, the resultant, is as destructive in all cases.

The actual confrontation in the forward areas of conflict, consisted of the heavy armament, which comprised howitzer artillery, the range of which was up to five miles and when the phosphorous shells were used at night, the sky would be illuminated so that it was easily visible for one hundred miles. This armament was used to shell any detectable position within the waddies, or on the mountain side, where any dissident element could be detected from air or ground observation posts.

Providing the daylight air spotting, or observation reconnaissance, was the Army Air Corps, in their small single engine Auster aircraft and at night the ground observers of the Federal Regular Army would provide information on any areas where a build up of enemy activity had been reported from their intelligence sources during the hours preceding darkness.

Radio communications were kept to a minimum for obvious reasons, as only line of sight VHF was effective in this mountainous terrain, which was satisfactory during daylight operations, when the Air Corps were directing activity from the sky, however, at night, only flashes of gun fire and detectable noises would identify enemy positions.

Personal hand to hand and small arms engagements were very few and far between, as planned incursions to suspected enemy positions, were too imprecise to be effective, as the movements of the enemy, would change from hour to hour, it was tantamount to a child playing in a backyard that was unfamiliar to him, where the playmate would have the advantage of the area geography, this, translated to a much larger scale in the mountains of South Yemen, where the tribesmen were 'playing on their home ground', which in the final analysis of military strategy, was akin to a superfluous exercise.

The Royal Air Force played the major role in the whole scenario, from logistic support and internal security to punitive excursions in the mountains, with both bomber and fighter sorties, day and night operations.

The two resident fighter squadrons, comprised of Hawker Hunter, single seat aircraft, the armament for which was two twenty millimeter cannon gun installations and wing mounted six inch rockets, both ordinance highly effective in air-to-ground offensive operations.

These squadrons were used ostensibly to strafe the enemy positions in the waddies and mountain strongholds after a strong presence of insurgents had been located by the observation aircraft. In some cases where a terrorist camp site or village had been spotted and was known to harbor a nucleus of dissidents who were causing havoc amongst the allied military units, a dawn attack on the position would be made by the fighters, which would facilitate a quick withdrawal of the incumbent tribesmen, disturbing their encampment, forcing a relocation of their hideout. This would only disrupt their nomadic lifestyle for a few days at a time, yet it was deemed necessary, by the military strategists, to keep the enemy on the move, precluding a build up of a more threatening cell of militia, ultimately foiling any planned incursions which might have been planned using the original position, as the base of operations.

Unconventional as the confrontation may be, military planning of offensive and defensive operations, had, of necessity, required conventional deployment of resources, as other alternatives had yet to be learned, given the special nature of the war zone. It was the input from the Federal Regular Army, with their comprehensive, detailed knowledge of the terrain and the inhabitants of the various regions, that gave some credibility to the military stratagem, at any given period of time. Hence it was a tremendous asset for the British Forces to have such knowledgeable people with which to consult on the local environment.

If for some geographical or environmental reasons, the dissident elements used small village settlements, from which to launch their terrorist attacks on the Protectorate, which was a frequent occurrence, at times of the year when the weather allowed, on the preceding day, the small transport aircraft, would fly over the designated area dropping leaflets to the civilian population, advising them of the upcoming demolition of their village or settlement, which would allow a timely evacuation of the area prior to any bombing activities. Although this appeared to be an unnecessary punitive action, it had the effect of alienating the terrorists from the resident villagers, thus creating a divisive situation amongst the Arab communities, which could only be favorable for the allied forces, in their efforts to eliminate areas from which the enemy could, hitherto, operate with impunity.

The third Hawker Hunter fighter element, was not an operational squadron in the sense that it was not used for offensive action, but rather for Photographic Reconnaissance, and was referred to as the PR Flight, the aircraft having specially adapted photographic equipment, suitably installed in the custom designed nose of the aircraft and used for high altitude surveillance activities. It was this additional spotting facility that allowed the forward offensive artillery in the mountains, to pinpoint enemy positions and dispatch suitable ordinance to those map coordinates. These particular aircraft could be de-modified, to allow ordinance to be fitted should the need arise, however as there was another squadron of fighters stationed in Salahla, in the Oman, just one hour's flying away from Aden and on immediate readiness, the need for the conversion would be remote indeed.

The small transport aircraft which were used to drop leaflets, to the hapless villages and to carry small volumes of cargo, were the Twin Pioneers, a twin radial engine aircraft, with a high lift wing and short field take-off capability, which could maintain low speed flight in all terrain, in fact when there was a high wind blowing down the runway, forward flight, at times was the exception, rather than the rule and to observers, at times, it would appear as if the aircraft were stationary. This aircraft was ideal for short strip landings and take-offs, especially in terrain where delicate or breakable cargo required an actual landing, prior to unloading, as it was a normal practice to deliver most loads from the air, by wooden pallets attached to which, was one or several parachutes, depending on the size of the load.

The heavy lift and high bulk loads were the responsibility of the two transport squadrons, which comprised of two types of four engine aircraft with completely separate roles.

Armstrong Whitworth Argosy's were logistically medium to long range transport aircraft, which plied their cargoes from The United Kingdom to the Aden

Protectorate and kept the normal supply lines open, supporting the military effort and at times transporting troops to Aden from various parts of the world. These aircraft were slow turbo-prop aircraft, the payload of which was not quite as much as one would expect, given the size of the aircraft, however it filled the slot in the absence of a more suitable alternative.

Beverlys were the second of the large transport aircraft, a huge, box-like aircraft, fitted with four large radial engines with propellers measuring eighteen feet in length, which were in all probability the largest of any heavy piston engine aircraft currently in service.

Heavy equipment, such as bulldozers and trucks could be carried to areas where the land forces required them and either delivered from the air by pallet and parachutes, as with the Twin Pioneers, but on a much larger scale, or given it's short field capability, could land and have the load dragged out of the cargo area by drogue shutes, using the forward momentum of the aircraft, without coming to a stop and before reaching the end of the landing field, take-off again.

This operation was normal procedure, however it did get rather hair raising in the valleys (waddies) where the runways were short and the ambient temperature close to one hundred degrees, making engine power that much more difficult to maintain on take off and climb out.

At times the Beverly could be used for carrying troops and equipment, or a combination of both heavy lift equipment and personnel, The tail boom of the aircraft carried approximately thirty fully equipped soldiers and had a door which could be opened to allow paratroopers to exit over a drop zone. It was an Elephant in the world of transport aircraft, but fulfilled its role adequately.

For offensive bombing missions, the heavy four engine Shackleton bomber was used. This squadron (37 Squadron) was very active during the hours of darkness for several reasons, which will be clarified in the following text. This bomber carried an assortment of ordinance, from twenty pound anti-personnel bombs, which could reap a heavy toll in confined areas, to the one thousand pound, ground leveling bombs, which were the more feared in the areas where the terrain was such that villages and stockades could be detected and easily demolished by these devastating weapons of destruction.

Night bombing was used in the forward areas of confrontation for two main reasons, the first being that the daylight photographic reconnaissance aircraft of the Hunter flight and the close spotting of the Army Air Corps Austers, could map out dissident positions and plot map references for the night assault.

Secondly, the Shackleton crews would fly over the mountainous areas during their nightly sorties and having delivered a partial bomb load to the prearranged map coordinates, they would fly, at a safe, low level altitude, conducive to the local terrain, to other areas where suspected enemy cells may be situated and would switch on all internal and external aircraft lights, which would attract sporadic gunfire from the ground, which once pinpointed, became the secondary target for the night's foray. Such impromptu bombing exercises were quite effective, which surprisingly, did nothing to suppress the exuberant tribesmen from shooting at the aircraft on a continual nightly basis, albeit with ancient muzzle loading rifles.

With all the combined air and ground activities, there was a twenty four hour spontaneous offensive activity, which tended to keep the enemy on the defensive and most military personnel on permanent shift work, which was not the most social of ways to conduct ones life, but nevertheless, was a necessary evil.

One helicopter squadron and a helicopter Search and Rescue flight made up the Air Force rotor wing compliment, at Royal Air Force Station, Khormaksar. The squadron, was made up of twin engine, twin rotor, cigar shaped helicopters, called Belvederes, which were used for heavy lift activities, moving supplies and munitions to the forward allied military positions, employing underslung cable and net apparatus to achieve the moving of bulky and vehicular loads.

The Search and Rescue (SAR) flight comprised single engine, single rotor, piston and turbo engine helicopters, yellow painted for easy identification, which, boded well for both friend and foe alike, yet at times, became an easy target for ground to air attack.

The SAR function, as always, was a humanitarian service, as it was employed for saving lives and did not discriminate between friend, foe, or civilian and I am proud to say that this was the entity to which I was attached and spent two years fulfilling a purposeful, active role. SAR was not the only role of these helicopters, as it was combined with the activities of Casualty Evacuation (CASAVAC) from the forward fighting areas and any emergency medical situation which might occur within the Protectorate, coupled with the onerous tasks of assisting the internal security forces on night patrols and moving smaller items of goods and equipment, to augment the Belvedere's logistical efforts.

Helicopter operations were essential for the efficient running of the military base and logistical support of the forward fighting zones, however, I was to learn that this specialized activity was fraught with unforeseen dangers, in all theaters of operation, both in the air and on the ground.

The Royal Navy played a substantial role in the logistical and manpower support of the military effort in Aden, however, their presence was spasmodic and required, only when the fighting or insurgencies escalated. On more than one occasion an aircraft carrier would anchor off Steamer Point and fly in replacement helicopters, aircraft engines and spare parts, together with any supplies which had been previously ordered by the military camps, distribution being through the supply depot at Khormaksar, as it was the largest and most secure area in the Protectorate.

Once, during my two year tenure in Aden, the Royal Navy supported the RAF by positioning a helicopter squadron at Khormaksar for a three month period, the job of which, was to support the lifting of heavy loads to the Army, situated in forward strategic positions in the Radfan mountains, this being accomplished, by the underslung loads, using the net and cable apparatus attached to the underside of the helicopters, the amount of pay load limited only by the size of the helicopter and its maximum operating lifting capacity.

The cooperation between all three services was excellent and through the ten years of military action in that theater of operations, the rapport was never in jeopardy, as all were of one accord, having a common goal and sharing common adversities, under extremely pernicious conditions.

Chapter Five

On my arrival in Aden, I was attached to the Search and Rescue (SAR) Helicopter Flight, as a Shift Leader, which meant that I had the responsibility of supervising several tradesmen during the course of their technical, general and administrative duties, encompassing, maintenance checks, aircraft preparation for missions, training and various change-of-role requirements, in fact everyone joined in all facets of the day or night operations, to create an effective readiness team for all eventualities.

Dawn to dusk was the SAR stand-by period, after which Internal security duties began. As we had three helicopters, we could fulfill more than the SAR duties during daylight hours and we would frequently be called upon to provide one for a casualty evacuation (CASAVAC) from the fighting zone, up country and at times for lifting supplies and personnel transportation. These requirements were part of the normal working day and the variety of assignments, made the working environment more interesting, as sometimes, duty personnel would accompany the helicopter, on the operation, to ensure all went well technically and to carry out refueling and security tasks.

Internal Security followed the stand down of the SAR stand-by and would take on a variety of duties depending on the military situation and requirements of the preceding day and as an operational convenience a separate helicopter would fulfill the role, otherwise it would mean changing all the SAR equipment for internal security equipment, which at times was impractical, due to time and available manpower constraints. Suffice to say that all helicopters were equipped to carry out any role. It was the loose equipment which had to be carried in each helicopter which made the difference as to the current role. Under normal circumstances, which in a war zone could change at a moments notice, one helicopter would be at SAR configuration, one at Internal Security readiness and one would be undergoing maintenance or modification work.

As SAR duty dictated, the watch involved the flight crew, listening out on the air and marine emergency radio frequencies and should a 'MAYDAY' or any distress call be made within the range of our radio receivers, a helicopter would be dispatched immediately to any coordinates given by the call for help, whether on land or sea.

We would frequently use the spare helicopter for practicing the various types of rescue mission, from personal sea rescues, when the flight crews from the various squadrons would be dropped into the sea, shark repellent et al, and would be extricated from the water, normally in order of rank, the seniors officers being first, leaving the junior officers until last, to the more mundane and leisurely exercises with the marine craft out at sea.All rescue exercises were accomplished by a winch and pulley system attached to the external frame of the helicopter and hydraulically powered, closely monitored by the flight crew and crew-man/winch operator..

The SAR helicopters operated with three flight crew, a pilot, a navigator (or second pilot) and a crewman. The crewman would be the person who would be attached to the winch hook by a suitable harness, the navigator operating the winch from the co-pilots, or cabin position, the pilot maintaining the helicopter at the hover, would be lowered to the person or equipment requiring to be lifted.

In the case of a sea rescue the crewman would execute a double lift, when he would ensure that the rescue harness (strop) was securely around the person to be rescued, he would wrap his legs around that person, at which time he would signal the winch man and both would be winched into the helicopter cabin. A double lift ensures a safer load on the end of the winch cable, where the additional weight would be less likely to swing, if the helicopter or high wind caused a lateral movement of the helicopter during the rescue operation, which was not uncommon in tropical climates, where the wind could blow up a storm instantaneously and catch the airmen unaware.

As previously stated, during a practice session of sea rescues for the flight crews, it was politic to extract the senior officer first and in most cases that was the acceptable protocol. On one occasion this was not the norm.

A junior officer SAR pilot, who, for his misfortune had been posted to a helicopter flight, having through all of his officer and flight training period, believed that he was destined to fly the latest technology fighter aircraft, with all its romantic connotations and grandiose accolades, suffered absolute deflation, when, under vociferous protest, he was assigned to a helicopter flight, convincing himself in retrospect, that negative forces were acting against his pursuit of a rightful place in the order of things ordained.

To create situations which would tend to accentuate his non acceptance of the status quo, the officer in question would bring attention to himself by making himself prominent in everyday normal operations, making the mundane duties the subject of scrutiny by all. This paranoid action, kept his name in the forefront of those who could and would influence his flying career, but did nothing to enhance his chances of promotion, for which, in essence, he did not want. His only reason for his anomalous behavior, was to maintain a constant affront to his peers and superiors, in the hope that he would either be reassigned or asked to resign his commission. To be absolutely unbiased, his performance as a SAR pilot was flawless and beneath his inflated ego, was a very personable man.

On this very bright, sunny, warm day, the sea rescue exercise for the pilots of the Hunter fighter squadron, was scheduled for mid morning, when the SAR helicopter would attempt the rescue operation in a very methodical, efficient, manner, it was however, a scenario for one man to seize a chance to further his notoriety in the minds of all who would bear witness to his exploits.

It was a fateful roster that assigned this particular pilot to the detail that would simulate the sea rescues, which could easily translate into actual events given the number of missions flown in one operational day, however with the complicity of both his navigator and crewman, events would unfold to create a more than humorous event, to those of us impartial enough to accept the inevitable.

Having been dropped into the Indian Ocean earlier that morning, several miles off shore, twelve airmen were being availed of the experience of surviving in a practical situation, drifting slowly in the easy swell of the warm sea. It would be a few hours before the rescue helicopter appeared and start the exercise, which would take at least two sweltering hours to complete, so other than watch for aquatic predators and soak up the infernal sun, they would of necessity have to be extremely patient.

Restricted to the number of people who could be carried at any one time, the SAR helicopter would probably make two or three journeys, from base, to the area of rescue, which would mean that the airmen who would be last on the list to be picked up, would spend an extra hour or two in the warm but rather dangerous sea, with all its predators.

Whales and dolphins were the harmless residents of the ocean. Sharks, sting rays, moray eels and barracuda were the creatures that would prey on flesh, should an opportunity present itself and they were not discriminatory in their dining habits, nor selective in the meal composition. This and many other unseen dangers could present themselves to the hapless pilots as they waited anxiously, adrift in the brine and foam of that great expanse of water.

Shark repellent and the basic survival equipment attached to their flying suits, were no deterrent from the lurking denizens of the deep, however, what could be more authentic than the real scenario. Little comfort to those who would be participating in the exercise.

At precisely noon, the SAR helicopter lifted off the landing pad and headed for the open sea to the assigned pick-up area, which after twenty minutes brought them within sight of the nearest airman floating warily, in what was now a choppy sea, the wind having become more brisk in the preceding half hour.

The nearest pilots to shore, historically, tended to be the last to be rescued, but today was different, the courtesy which would normally be extended to those bobbing around in the far distance, was not about to be a consideration by the pilot of the rescue helicopter. Rank did not enter the equation, nor did the philosophy of granting the more senior mature airmen, an expeditious removal from this undignified situation.

As the helicopter circled the luckless pilots, it was apparent that the search was of a more personal nature and the pilot who had been given the rescue mission was enjoying every minute of his present folly, being played out in the middle of the Indian Ocean.

Spotting the Squadron Commander swirling around in the foam, the helicopter pilot hovered above him on the pretense that he was about to be rescued, this however was not to be. At a prearranged signal, the navigator attached himself to the winch hook and ably assisted by the winch operator descended to the waiting officer. At approximately three feet from the now smiling rescuee, the navigator removed from his flying suit, what appeared to be a small booklet and stretching out to the ranking officer, gave it to the bemused man in the sea. At a further prearranged signal from the pilot to the winch operator, the navigator was pulled back up to the helicopter cabin and once inside, the helicopter banked steeply and headed out to sea. At a later date, it was ascertained that the booklet given to the Squadron Commander on that brief and rather bizarre rescue mission, was an official Air Force Manual, entitled, 'Sea Survival'

Needless to say the formal repercussions of the previous event were minimal, as there is no code of conduct regulating the way in which rescue missions should be carried out, however, to ignore accepted protocol in a world of ones peers,not-to-mention, the Officers Club, was tantamount to professional suicide. Several months later the helicopter pilot in question, was posted to another helicopter assignment, in the same theater of operations but in a more rural and inhospitable area, at least a thousand miles from Aden. It is commonly referred to as being 'Hung by your own Petard' or Poetic justice.

Chapter Six

The Belvedere helicopters had a love-hate relationship with all who had any dealings with the machine, it was in many ways a temperamental beast, a work horse with many idiosyncrasies, excellent when all combinations of man, machine and environment were in synchronism, but a potential death trap when any one element was awry.

During a normal operational sortie to the forward battle positions in the Radfan Mountains, where an infantry regiment had established a base camp, a supply run had been organized to deliver fresh vegetable produce and a Belvedere was allocated for this particular task, due to its high load capacity and underslung load capabilities. As the bulk of the load was several bushels of onions it was, as always, packaged and placed in the net, which constituted the underslung load.

With the cabin fully laden with fresh fruit and assorted vegetables the helicopter lifted off to a height of six to eight feet and hovered over the net which was quickly attached to the cable and hook assembly under the craft, by the ground crew. This accomplished, the helicopter increased the engine power and steadily gained altitude as it sped towards the mountainous drop zone.

Flying over the various peaks and valleys en route to the rendezvous the helicopter encountered many thermals, which at the best of times created moderate turbulence and at other times made the airborne quality of the Belvedere, similar to that of a manhole cover, which over a decade of operations had taken its toll of human life.

This particular sortie had a conclusion, which any movie Director would have given a year's salary to capture on film. As the helicopter descended in to the drop zone, heavy turbulence was encountered at approximately two thousand feet and the underslung load started to swing like a giant pendulum. As the arc of the swing increased the pilot struggled with the controls, in an effort to gain some lateral stability, it was however, a vain attempt at regaining stabilized flight and the pendulum continued its ever-increasing swinging arc.

Any attempt at arresting a twin rotor helicopter, once it has become unstable in the longitudinal axis, only tended to increase the instability as the pilots had a tendency to overcorrect, which aggravated an already irrecoverable situation.

There comes a point where a decision, vital to the welfare of man and machine, must, of necessity be made, at which point the winch man or the pilot could activate an explosive charge and sever the cable holding the under-slung load. In this particular situation the pilot triggered the action and a very heavy load of onions was scattered throughout the length of the valley, the odor from which was reported to have lingered for several weeks and precipitated the redeployment of the Regimental base camp.

In a completely separate incident, after completing a bombing mission, in the forward areas of the war zone, a Royal Navy fighter bomber, had an engine flame-out whilst returning to the Aircraft Carrier, Ark Royal, in the Indian Ocean As the range to the aircraft carrier was greater than the distance to the nearest airfield, the pilot declared a "May Day" emergency situation and immediate clearance to land at Khormaksar airfield was given by the Air Traffic Controllers.

This situation, which was in essence a full emergency, as the aircraft was descending into the runway with, what is termed, a 'dead stick', which necessitated a landing without any engine control. After a long approach and a great deal of skillful airmanship, the fighter glided on to the runway. After touch down with minimal braking ability, the aircraft came to a stop, without any injury to the pilot or aircraft. This was assuredly an excellent piece of airmanship and one that could not be duplicated easily.

As the spare engine for the aircraft, was in store on the aircraft carrier, which was standing off several miles out to sea, a Belvedere was dispatched to pick it up, which again required an underslung load situation.

As heavy as the engine was, the helicopter was quite capable of lifting and transporting the load over a long distance and once picked up, the engine, which was housed in a large wooden transport container, was carried under the helicopter to the Air Force base, where, the stricken aircraft awaited its replacement engine.

As the helicopter approached the designated spot, adjacent to the hangar in which the engine replacement was to take place, a strong gust of wind, which came from the desert and swept across the main runway blasting its way between the hangars, causing an updraft, which created a vortex and in a very short time started the load swinging on its cable.

As the load increased its swing, gaining momentum with every pendulous movement, the pilot tried to gain altitude to move away from the dangerous drafts, however in doing so caused the load to move even further from the perpendicular.

Finally the swinging motion of the heavy load overcame the efforts of the pilot to neutralize the unnatural aerodynamic forces exerted on his helicopter and without further ado, he instructed his winch man to actuate the cable cutting mechanism and the engine struck the hard tarmac at a high rate of knots, the g forces from which, cracked open the wooden packing case, hurling the four thousand pound engine on a trajectory which ultimately destroyed it beyond repair.

Fortunately the engine fell into an open space adjacent to the perimeter taxi way, so there were no injuries to personnel on the ground, the debris was strewn across an extensive area, which had to be immediately cordoned off for the subsequent, inevitable military inquiry and predictable recriminations against those whose job it was to carry out the assigned detail.

Needless to say the Fleet Air Arm of the Royal Navy were not too happy about the destruction of a very expensive, not to mention very important item, the replacement of which would take several weeks, which in an attempt to partially atone for the untimely mishap, the Royal Air Force accepted the logistic responsibility and transported a replacement engine from the United Kingdom in an Argosy transport aircraft, which arrived within two weeks of the accident.

Given the high degree of responsibility, the inherent instability of the Belvedere helicopter and the frequently changing environmental conditions, the pilot was given no alternative as to his actions. Safety of personnel is paramount in any given situation and to err on the side of safety is undeniably the correct and ethical approach to the emergencies, which confront the pilots and flight crews on a daily basis.

Another episode in the ever topical escapades of the Belvedere, happened in a very remote area of the Radfan mountain range where dissident elements were known to be operating and launching frequent offensive operations against the security forces.

This area was known to have supported a number of tribes whose specialties were the setting of ambushes and the laying of mines on access roads, which made cautious approached an imperative, it was however, a situation where not all eventualities could be covered at any given instance and many soldiers were killed or maimed as a result of these wanton, flagrant acts of terrorism.

To pursue the eradication of the dissident element in the area of concern, the Army Air Corps patrolled the skies above the immediate locale, reporting to the field commanders as necessary and maintaining a constant visual daylight presence, to preclude the build up of opposing factions, prior to an incursion into the area for a clean up operation.

Flying the single engine Auster aircraft which the Army Air Corps used for Air Observation Posts (AOP) which basically, was the spotting of enemy positions and heavy ordinance to allow the allied forces artillery to home in on the site and destroy it, without having to employ ground troops and heavy transport, which in such terrain would be slow, cumbersome and in all respects, dangerous.

These light aircraft were at times very difficult to handle in the waddies and ravines, due to the thermals which were sometimes accompanied by swift updrafts, creating swirling vortices, which would toss the little aeroplane around the skies like a bottle cork on a rising tide.

It was some such a day that the pilot of the spotter plane ventured too low in an effort to detect the highly camouflaged enemy position, when a very strong gust of wind lifted a wing to an attitude which made flight impossible, the small aircraft hit the side of the rocky ravine and came to a very abrupt and ignominious stop. The pilot was very fortunate to walk away from the crash with no more than a broken ego, however, the aircraft remained in a very precarious position, where recovery would be most difficult.

A Belvedere helicopter was dispatched to the scene of the crash to assist in extricating the stricken craft. Soon it was positioned over the site and the winch man descended into the area on the winch hook and began to attach a lifting strop around the fuselage of the Auster. This accomplished, he gave the signal to the pilot to start the lift and ascend in a vertical manner to ensure maximum clearance for the load, as it would have to navigate rocky out-croppings as it was lifted into a position where transition to forward flight would be possible.

As the aircraft was slowly lifted out of its would-be incarceration, the pilot of the Belvedere, unsighted by the mass of rocks and the fact that a vertical lift did not allow him a panoramic view of his load, made a marginal error, as his only reference to the direction to which he must position the helicopter, was through the intercom system, where instructions from the winch man guided his actions.

At the very point where the Auster would have cleared all obstructions in its ascent to freedom, a slight deviation from the vertical by the Belvedere, which in no way could be avoided, as the helicopter was subjected to many various thermals and air movements on its ascent, the wing tip of the Auster touched the top of a protruding rocky knoll, which caused the aircraft to swivel on it horizontal axis, causing, the pilot of the Belvedere to adjust his ascent, turning it into an unstable air current, precipitating a swinging movement of the load, this in turn created the situation in which many helicopter pilots find themselves, when trying to neutralize an abnormal flight situation. The action of the pilot correcting the swinging load, only exacerbated the situation and the load continued to swing in that ever increasing pendulous motion, until finally the momentum of the load, jeopardized the safety of the Belvedere and the pilot made the decision to sever the cable which held the doomed Auster aircraft.

Dropping any aircraft form a height of five hundred feet, without the means of self propulsion, leads to an inevitable conclusion, which the Army Air Corps in no way appreciated, especially when it reduced the size of its observation fleet by one half. Accidents do occur and in many cases are unavoidable when the environment is hostile and unforgiving. This is perhaps the price of conducting a war effort, however honorable, in very foreign and unfamiliar parts of the world, where the slightest deviation from the familiar, can mean the difference between the ordinary and disaster.

The final chapter in the saga of the Belvedere helicopter, is one of the unacceptable face of, coincidence, trauma and fatality, a combination of the most pernicious order.

A routine early morning sortie to the forward most positions occupied by the duty regiment, which at the time was the Royal Scots Regiment, delivered supplies of ordinance, perishable food stuff and two soldiers rejoining their colleagues after spending a most uncomfortable two weeks in an RAF Hospital in the Protectorate, which to a veteran squaddie (British Soldier) was tantamount to consorting with the enemy, a situation which did not go unnoticed by their fellow combatants and would be the source of much jocular railing in the ensuing few days.

Having delivered the load, the helicopter quickly departed the drop zone and headed towards base at a rate of knots that could never be sustained with a high gross pay load, but would get the crew back to their quarters in time for a late lunch.

Crossing an area which was a known enemy small arms fire zone and while attempting to increase altitude as quickly as a twin rotor helicopter is able, a plume of smoke from the ground heralded the launching of a hand held missile which quickly acquired the track of the aircraft and in an attempt to avoid the oncoming projectile, the pilot banked the helicopter sharply to the right, which presented the underside of the aircraft to the missile allowing a perfect target area for the detonation.

Shuddering violently, with the effect of the explosive power of the missile, the helicopter was thrown into a precarious attitude, which, without the extreme expertise of the veteran pilot, would have foundered and crashed.

Bringing the helicopter under control the pilot pulled on as much collective pitch as the airframe would sustain to gain altitude and avoid any further missile attacks. It was however, a fruitless action, as the explosive power of the missile had penetrated the main fuel tank, the penetration being completely through to the main cabin of the Belvedere, which quickly became awash with jet fuel.

The crewman, who was positioned in the main cabin, adjacent to the open door, could not retreat far enough into the recesses of the cabin, his restraint being his safety line attached to his body harness, to prevent fuel from soaking his flying suit and with a terror that can only be experienced by someone awaiting the spark which would incinerate him, he screamed through his throat microphone to the pilots for help, which, had common sense been allowed to prevail, could in no way be made available, as the pilots were in no position to help themselves, due to the desperate fight they were having in an endeavor to control a crippled helicopter, let alone unseat themselves and lower themselves into a potential death trap.

When the crewman had regained his composure and emotion had been nullified, the three crew members discussed the situation and quickly came to a decision to create a basic plan for the survival of themselves and the helicopter. An emergency call was made to the Air Traffic Control at Khormaksar, detailing the nature of the emergency and the proposed track to be taken on the approach and landing phase.

The basic plan was to fly the aircraft back to base, fuel quantity permitting and make an approach from over the sea which would provide for a back up plan if they had to ditch prior to making landfall, which in the event, would preclude the potential of fire but would not auger good for the survival prospects of the crew. The contingency plan for the crewman was for him to jump out at about ten feet above the ground and roll clear, before the helicopter touched down, this would obviate any chance of him being caught in a fire trap should a stray spark ignite the fuel in the cabin.

Isolating the ruptured fuel tank by a mechanical mechanism, comprising an operating lever and cable pulley system actuated by the co-pilot, the remaining fuel in the auxiliary tank seemed adequate to allow them to reach the airfield, although with very little in reserve.

Finally, the airfield came into sight, which meant that another ten miles would see them in a relatively safe haven. The pre-arranged landing area had been designated as a flat open desert strip, in the center of the airfield, far enough away from any built up area or from any aircraft hangars and parking bays. Emergency fire and medical vehicles would be positioned at a suitable distance from the designated area, allowing immediate access to any untoward event within a one mile radius.

Final preparations having been made, a slow turning circle was initiated which would bring the helicopter half a mile out to sea and allow a gradual descent on to the landing strip, almost another half mile from the coast line.

The subsequent sequence of events is not all that clear and could only be speculated upon at a future time when an official inquiry would be convened.

At a point just over the shore-line, the helicopter initiated a turn, which would bring it into wind and hopefully assist the flare and landing phases. At about a five degree bank angle the yaw cable snapped and all lateral stability was lost which made controlled flight almost impossible. Coincident with this anomaly was a flame out on the primary engine and the standby engine failed to spool up and assume the load of the main rotor heads drive and gear box which the now defunct power plant had divested itself.

Without the means of sustaining forward flight the aircraft plummeted to the ground where on impact the oleos (landing gear) bottomed out and the forward rotor head droop stops failed to arrest the downward motion of the blades, two of which snapped off on the first impact.

At about ten feet above the ground on its downward descent, the crewman jumped clear of the helicopter and rolled clear of the rotor blade arc and quickly shrugged off his fuel drenched flying suit and turned to face the stricken helicopter, hoping he would be in a position to assist his fellow airmen if the opportunity arose.

As the oleos (landing gear struts) hit bottom of their travel, the natural laws of physics prevailed and the helicopter rebounded into the air to about seven feet. It was at this point that the unknown source of ignition occurred and flames were soon shooting out of the engine cowlings and instantly propagated to the fuel soaked cabin.

As the helicopter settled on the hard packed earth, the two pilots, conscious of the dire situation they were in, tried to mechanically open the Perspex canopy of the cockpit, to no avail. Their efforts were redoubled in the ensuing seconds and they could be seen struggling, arms flailing, in a panic stricken effort to release their only exit from the inferno.

Fire engines and ambulances were only a few hundred yards away, sirens and bells heralding their approach, which through no fault of their own were too slow, too far.

Within seconds of the fire spreading to the helicopter cabin, the heat became so intense that any approach to within ten yards was impossible. Flames totally engulfed the helicopter and the fated two crew members died in their seats, before any remedial action could be taken by the fire tenders. The agonizing screams of the dying men entombed in their fiery coffin will forever live in the memories of those who had the misfortune to witness the demise of two brave airmen.

Chapter Seven

Search and Rescue operations are a continuous part of a theater of war and a very important aspect of moral stability for the soldiers, sailors and airmen whose job it is to confront the foe and suffer the mortal ramifications of military combat. To have the knowledge that at a moments notice, help and support is just a radio call away, where dedicated professionals stand ready to pit their skills against all odds and elements to succor those in pain or peril, is indeed a comforting thought.

It is sixty miles and one thousand feet above sea level, from the Port of Aden to the foothills of the Radfan mountain range and as the base operation for the SAR flight was too far from the areas of conflict, to allow expeditious recovery operations, the decision was made to establish a temporary base camp in a strategic area, situated in a remote, yet flat, sandy expanse, nestling in a well appointed location, in the foothills of the Jebel Radfan, surrounded on the north, east and west by high rock formations and to the south by open desert. `The name of the place was Thamier

Light plant and equipment were brought up from the Protectorate and a daily roster was set up for those whose duties were to keep the camp in a fully prepared active unit.

A Whirlwind helicopter was positioned at Thamier, for routine flights to the forward positions, supporting the heavy artillery units with men and supplies, other times, standing at a moments readiness for casualty evacuation (casavac) of the wounded, for immediate transportation to Aden, Steamer Point, Hospital. When such an event occurred, a replacement helicopter was dispatched from Aden to Thamier to ensure a continuous essential service to those who relied on the SAR flight.

Several very poignant and bizarre events were to take place in the space of a six month period in 1964, all of which had a lasting, significant influence on the political and military presence in the Republic of South Yemen.

The first narrative involved a well respected and popular Army Officer, a man totally immersed in his chosen career, an athlete, a scholar and a dutiful son of a well known military family, applauded by his superiors, peers and subordinates as a role model for those young men and women who would be part of a military heritage.

I had the fortune to meet Captain Peter Garfield-Smith during my years as a rugby football player with the Air Force, Peter representing his Regiment and the British Army and I representing my Base and the Royal Air Force.

As an infantry officer, it was frequently incumbent upon him to be positioned in the forward fighting areas, which we commonly referred to as up-country.

It was on one of these occasions that his regiment was in an offensive front line area, that he found himself rostered for Duty Officer, a duty which he had performed many times previously and entailed checking the many items of daily field activities, including, posting and periodically visiting the sentry positions.

During the hours of daylight, it was a relatively easy task to do the rounds of the sentry positions, where identification of personnel could be easily established, as military protocol dictated, a formal challenge and reply regimen be carried out, irrespective of the time of day or night. There is however no substitute for a clear view in the light of day, when identities can be established at a glance.

The Duty Officer's watch, lasted a full twenty four hours, from seven o'clock in the morning, the vigil being a rather tiring and boring affair, unless the encampment came under attack, which was not likely, as all base camps were strategically situated and would be difficult to compromise, unless under air attack and the enemy had no significant Air Force with which to mount any offensive.

This night as darkness fell, Peter Garfield-Smith prepared for the long night of duty starting with an inspection of the soldiers mess tent, spending a considerable time talking with the non-commissioned ranks, joking and asking for any complaints, which in itself was always a joke and always took the form of the ever present military banter which bespoke the kind of camaraderie, which existed in most regular army units, employed in combat zones.

Breaking away from the mess tent, he decided to carry out a patrol of the sentry positions, before dinner, which would give him some respite after eating, allowing him the luxury of catching up on his mail and seven day old newspapers from England.

Taking a path, which would lead him to the furthermost sentry post, he navigated his way around rocky knolls and rough stony pathways, he approached the first sentry post.

At a distance of one hundred yards, the soldier on duty challenged the Officer, as regulations dictated. As the distance between sentry and Duty Officer, precluded the formal recognition process, albeit, the night being clear and moonlit, identification of any approaching person to a designated sentinel must, of necessity, be positively established.

The formal challenge having been made in a very distinct, loud voice, the sentry awaited the reply, which constituted the daily password, of which all duty personnel should be aware. If a reply to a challenge is not forthcoming, the challenge must be repeated, which in this particular case, from all subsequent reports, did occur. To this day, it is not known why a diligent, duty-minded officer, the likes of Peter Garfield-Smith, did not respond to the challenge in the prescribed manner, instead, he replied by stating his name and rank, an answer which the sentry could not accept.

Perhaps as with all mortals, Garfield-Smith had a temporary lapse of memory and his inability to recall the password was a mental aberration, the substance of which remains inexplicable to those whose clinical studies encompasses the cerebral intricacies of the human mind.

The sentry, unable to disseminate duty from common sense, presented his weapon in the appropriate manner and continued the challenge. Being young and relatively inexperienced, not wanting to show his shortcomings to his superiors, not wanting to fail in his avowed and sworn duty, regulations were the only resource to which he could turn and to his credit as a soldier, he maintained the rigid thought processes, which, in all military codes of ethics could not be faulted.

Having endeavored to elicit a response to his challenge and finding no acceptable reply, the soldier removed the safety from his weapon and aimed at the approaching officer, the distance from both men must have been such that neither could identify the other and one could surmise that the sentry presented with this untenable situation carried out his duty to the ultimate degree. At a much later date the Board of Inquiry could not ascertain the exact state of mind of the sentry, however, no fault could be apportioned to that dutiful soldier.

Peter Garfield-Smith died on that fateful night, killed by a sentry from his own Company, by a man who had the greatest respect for his officer and even more respect for his uniform and the British Army to which he had owed and given his allegiance.

A search and rescue helicopter was immediately made ready for the evacuation of the dead officer to the Aden Protectorate where in due course, the body was transshipped to the United Kingdom for a ceremonial burial at the family country estate.

Due to the delicate nature of the situation, the sentry, for his own safety, was immediately removed from his unit and sent back to the United Kingdom to answer a formal investigation. The disposition of this young soldier was never known, perhaps, to enable him to remain in anonymity with his conscience and dire memories.

To philosophize on the whole sad affair would only be speculative, as to the reasons why men should react in a certain way to certain situations. Perhaps the eulogy on the man who died would be suffice to allay the pondering of those who would decry one human frailty of one mortal man.

Chapter Eight

To dwell too long on the happenings in a war stricken region, where turmoil, hate, economic and social inequalities abound, can only detract from the human element, which in reality, is that which provokes all altercation and dissent in an ever volatile world.

One very alive and vibrant story, evolves around a man with whom I was associated for two very long and uncomfortable years, in the land of sand, rocks, interminable humidity and scorching heat, known as Aden.

Flight Lieutenant Walton-Hadley was my Flight Commander for my period of duty in Aden, a man of very high integrity, exceptional flying abilities and a decorated war veteran, whose medals included the Air Force Cross and Distinguished Flying Cross, two medals of honor, bestowed only upon the most brave and deserving of men.

He was a man of many parts, a disciplinarian, a pragmatist, a good husband and father and one who many would say, was an exception to the rule that "Pigs can't Fly". His mannerisms were terse and sometimes bordered on the verbally abusive, but never in a way that could be legitimately construed as pernicious.

Walton-Hadley's exploits as a military pilot were widely renowned and in many circles revered, in both the fixed and rotary wing environment. As a flight instructor his success was unequaled, which in later life was to stand him in good stead when his Air Force career finally came to an end and he entered civilian life to continue in aviation, giving back something to the profession in which he excelled, imparting his experience and knowledge to many young and in some cases, mature airline pilots, who had the misfortune to have missed the intractable discipline of a military training which creates a basic stable character on which to build a formidable operator of flying machines.

On occasion, Walton-Hadley could be charming, compassionate, witty and calculating, but in all instances, genuine and forthright.

My recollection of his demeanor comes in many guises and there were several poignant happenings, that truly showed his salient characteristics.

On a morning sortie preparation, the three crew were sitting in the helicopter, engines running, rotors turning, awaiting ATC (Air Traffic Control) clearance to taxi and take-off, when C. Walton-Hadley, motioned to me that he wanted to speak with our illustrious Line Chief, Flight Sergeant Pruitt, the reason for which at the time eluded me, but was none of my business. I duly jogged to the line office and informed the Chief that the Boss wanted to speak with him.

Now, the Chief was a rather short, pudgy, fellow and not at all athletic and to an experienced independent observer, would appear rather short on basic common sense and a little backward in the workings of the very aircraft, the care of which he was charged.

Extracting his pipe from his mouth, the Chief laid it lovingly on his desk, this action was a daily ritual when he had to leave his office, it was generally thought that he smoked the pipe to project a more manly, macho image to all around, which might tend to negate, however minimally, his lack of physical stature. Moving at a speed which was conducive to his thought processes, he emerged from the crew shack and ambled down to the hard standing where the helicopter was now at a pre take-off state, rotors at a constant rpm with the attendant gentle rocking of the fuselage, which was a normal situation, due to the gyroscopic nature of the rotor movement, transferring the torque through an imperfectly balanced vehicle, which sometimes became totally unstable and necessitated a quick transition from ground to flight. This condition is known as 'ground resonance'.

Reaching the right hand side of the helicopter, the Chief proceeded to climb to the cockpit using the foot and hand holds. As he ascended to a level adjacent to the pilot's position, he seemed to continue his upward movement and precisely as his head passed the top structure of the cockpit, a hand came out of the cockpit, with such speed that it almost knocked the chief off his perch, pulling him laterally through the cockpit opening, where he ended up lying prostrate across the lap of the Boss, whose quick action prevented a very messy decapitation of the Chief by the main rotors.

From where I observed the event, unable to do anything to prevent the potential disaster due to the noise of the engine, the margin by which a most horrible event was avoided, was inches. The quick action of Walton-Hadley, undoubtedly, saved the life of Flight Sergeant Pruitt who somewhat bemused by the whole event, took the rest of the day off.

Another, more personal story concerning my Flight Commander, happened when he called me prior to an evening stand down, to tell me that he needed a SAR helicopter at first light the following morning, for a sortie up country and he wanted me to be in attendance and indeed accompany him to our base camp (Thamier) at the foot hills of the Radfan mountain range. He emphasized that the helicopter should be fully equipped, as for a full SAR stand-by, with particular emphasis on the three bullet proof vests for the crew, one of which would be for yours truly.

Promptly, next day, at first light I presented myself at the armory to draw my personal weapon, which in this instance was a sterling sub-machine gun, not much use for firing from a helicopter, but certainly more compact and more easily handled in confined spaces. It was essentially a close quarters weapon designed for house to house searches where pin point accuracy was not the order of the day, however, for the particular purpose which I had in mind, which was not mortal combat, it suited very well, fulfilling my obligation to carry a weapon as the boss had directed.

My preferred weapon was the Belgian FN SLR, but again was too cumbersome to carry in a helicopter. The pilot and navigator carried side-arms which in the main consisted of the antique thirty eight revolver, which was not the fire power one would wish to have in a tight situation, but was light and compact.

Having ensured that the SAR stand-by helicopter was fully up to the required state for normal duties, I applied myself to the task of making the second aircraft suitably equipped for the coming journey up country.

I personally placed the three bullet-proof vests in the aircraft and returned to my normal duties until the Flight Commander was ready to take off, at which time I would join the crew in my capacity this day, as crewman.

I was called about thirty minutes later when the boss and the navigator had completed their pre-flight checks, then handing over the shift responsibilities to my deputy, I hopped aboard the helicopter and attached the safety harness to my person and sat in the most comfortable position with my feet and legs overhanging the door way, the door being latched fully open, this gives a very good panoramic view of the terrain to the right hand side of the aircraft and I had in previous flights had magnificent views of whales, sharks, manta rays and many other sea creatures in the Indian Ocean.

We took off and headed across the desert toward the mountains, which was approximately seventy miles, after which we would negotiate a few waddies before arriving at base camp. Once airborne and safely at our cruising speed and altitude, I realized that I did not have on, my bullet proof vest and I proceeded to cast my eyes around the cabin expecting to see it lying in the corner, but it was nowhere to be seen. At this point I plugged in my intercom and squeezing the throat microphone, asked the pilot if he knew where the elusive vest might be. To try and characterize the reply, which came back to me, would not be in the best interests of this passage of literature.

Suffice to say, that the third vest was protecting part of the anatomy of the Flight Commander, which if penetrated by a bullet or some such projectile, would cause much grief, not only to him, but to the navigator and myself and would definitely impair the safety of the helicopter.

This was communicated to me in a choice vernacular, suitably punctuated with epithets not becoming an officer and a gentleman. I accepted the inevitable and made the best of the remaining journey, hoping that the dissident element on the ground was not having a good day with their cannons or whatever they might be pointing at us, this beautiful morning.

In summary, I can attest to the fact that C. Walton-Hadley was as strict a disciplinarian with all whom he commanded, officers and ordinary airman alike and was indeed an airman of extraordinary talents, as will be typified in further accounts of a life in Aden.

Chapter Nine

During the latter half of 1964, the political situation for all intents and purposes, had not improved and the British Government, in all their wisdom, could not come to terms with the existing situation, even with all the recommendations from the Governor General and the incumbent Military Commanders.

There had been several visits from England of Ministers from the Foreign Office (FO) and Ministry of Defense (MOD), notably a Deputy Prime Minister of the period, who, with a grandiose entourage of local Arab dignitaries and British and FRA Military Commanders, embarked on a one-day survey of the war zone. He was flown, by helicopter, to a plateau in the Radfan mountain range, where he enjoyed a panoramic, breathtaking view of the mountain range, a luxurious lunch in an air conditioned tent, after which he was flown back to the Protectorate to continue private talks with the Governor General and Senior Military Commanders.

It was a few weeks before the residents of Aden, through the news media, was appraised of the findings from this auspicious visit, summed up, by the Deputy Prime Minister assuring the British Parliament that the Middle East conflict was well contained and that he was in full control of the situation, a proclamation, given the reality of the status quo, was met by a consensus of derision, by all who endured the daily rigors of life in the deserts of the Arabian Peninsular.

To further exacerbate the frustration of the civil and military leaders in Aden, several events, precipitated by the incumbent British Government of the day, made the intolerable situation worse and was manifest in ways which would inflame even the more modestly serene people.

One such event, which will remain in the memories of those who served in the middle-east, was precipitated by a local official communiqué, issued by the General Officer Commanding (GOC) ground troops, to the MOD in London.

The nub of the report, outlined the fact, that when any of the allied military personnel were captured or killed by the dissident faction in the war zone, they were tortured in hideous ways and after their demise, were mutilated, by being decapitated and their genitals sewn into their mouths, which throughout the annals of history, had been the symbolic way for the Arab world to show their utter contempt for their enemies. This report was a sober, factual account of daily occurrences in the republic of South Yemen, one, which was to be the center of attention for a protracted period of time.

During a Parliamentary session in the British House of Commons, the subject of Aden was broached by a former military officer, a representative of a conservative constituency, in rural England.His question to the Defense Minister inquired as to the ethics of the Arab dissidents and why could they not allow the bodies of the dead to be buried in the proper prescribed manner of a dead warrior.

Replying to the question, the Defense Minister prevaricated and could not give a definitive answer, as he did not know the full circumstances of the situation and promised that he would investigate the report form the GOC Aden.

At this juncture, a certain lady member of the Cabinet, was recognized by the Speaker of the House, as she wished to make a statement on the subject matter. Summarizing, her statement and allowing for the embellishments that all politicians are wont to use, the main thrust, pontificated on the absolutely unwarranted assail on the Arab nations and their purported acts of depraved butchery, castigating the GOC for making such libelous and insensitive remarks, which in her estimation were unfounded and unsubstantiated and in her mind in no way portrayed the acts of the dissident tribesmen, indeed she alleged that the comments of the GOC were a flagrant attempt to inflame an already volatile situation. Having said her piece, she resumed her seat on the Government bench.

Reports of the speech by the Right Honorable Lady, were seen in all daily newspapers and television media, which would not filter through to the military Commanders in Aden for at least two days, given the time differences and the bureaucratic procedures of Government dispatches to the more remote outposts of the Empire. Radio reception in the middle east was in either Arabic or some other dialect not easily recognizable by the English speaking community, the BBC World Service being somewhat transient in its broadcasts and in many cases, due to natural global phenomena, difficult to receive, news was always late.

Once the word had filtered through to the Governor General and the Military Commanders, there was much concern that the Government of the day must have misconstrued and misunderstood the transcripts. The official reports were an objective matter of fact and not something to be derided by the poorly informed, poorly advised ministerial personnel. 'A little knowledge is a dangerous thing', a maxim which all in the 'Halls of Power' should heed when making summary declarations on areas in which they had, to say the least, minimal experience.

To say the GOC Land Forces was somewhat perturbed by the latest revelations, would be vastly understating the situation and he decided, together with his senior subordinates, to put the whole affair into some perspective. To this end he proposed a reconnaissance mission into the area where the bodies of the allied soldiers were reported to have been mutilated and buried, intelligence sources of the FRA having conducted due diligence in the subject area and made a rough map of the more likely burial grounds.

Helicopters, of necessity, would have to be employed in the proposed mission and because the terrain was rugged and not much known of the surface conditions, the lightest and more maneuverable helicopters were chosen for the job, namely the SAR aircraft, which for the record were single engine Westland Whirlwind helicopters.

Preparations were made in a timely fashion and secrecy was the order of the day, as it would be ironic should a reception committee be waiting for the insurgents on a mission in enemy territory, not to mention the potential for losing two helicopters, were a fire fight to break out in uncomfortably confined spaces.

A dawn departure was ordered for the following day and two helicopter crews were assembled, together with ten fully equipped members of the Paratroop Regiment, five for each aircraft and two FRA officers, one in each helicopter respectively. After take off, the helicopters flew low over the desert region and headed for foothills of the Radfan mountain range, where several tricky flying maneuvers were carried out to allow the terrain to be traversed with the least likelihood of detection by elements of the hostile warring factions.

Arriving at the appointed map coordinates the helicopters landed where a suitable, clear, flat area was perceived and the soldiers disembarked and took up defensive positions at a pre-designated perimeter.

The two FRA officers were quickly at work, looking for tell tale signs of what might be fresh graves and it was not long before a grizzly discovery was made, very close to a rocky over-hang some fifty meters from where the landing site was established, the graves having been very shallow in nature, made the find an easy one. Amongst the soil and rocky debris, two human heads, the ethnic origins of which were obvious, were found laying in very close proximity to each other. A further search of the near vicinity, produced the emaciated torsos of what could only have been the remains of the headless British soldiers.

Two heavy fabric, body sacks, were brought from the helicopters and with great care, the cadavers, together with the human heads were placed inside and both sealed and then returned to the aircraft for transportation back to the protectorate.

The whole exercise from touch down to take off was perhaps ten minutes, made thus, by the excellent reconnaissance work previously carried out by the FRA, allowing no extraneous time to be consumed in the clock-work-like operation.

Once back in the confines of the airfield, the human remains were unloaded and shipped to a previously arranged destination, where the rights of the individuals would not be violated by over zealous news reporters. Later it would be learned,that the dismembered bodies were photographed and copies sent via Diplomatic Bag, to the United Kingdom, for onward transmission to the Right Honorable Lady, in the House of Commons. The bodies in question were finally given a Christian burial, befitting members of Her Majesty's Armed Forces. It was never definitely established, whether or not the Lady in question actually saw the photographs, it was however, known, that she was verbally appraised of them, but true to her colors, she in no way, shape, or form, offered an apology, publicly or otherwise to the GOC Aden Land Forces.

It must be a wonderful achievement to be so enlightened as to become an expert in all things political, or indeed apolitical, to pontificate on highly sensitive and controversial matters, where objectivity is a by-word, and truth, a contemptible misnomer, the qualifications for which, are a seat in the House of Commons and an utter contempt for human dignity.

As an aside, the Lady in question was eventually made a Dame of the British Empire, for what, only conjecture and fate knows, however this allowed her to sit in the elevated Peerage of The House of Lords from there to further pontificate on subjects various, most of which she had very limited knowledge, but can, by her lofty position effect the lives of those who live by their word and deed.

Chapter Ten

Perhaps the most vivid memory of the field operations in Aden, happened in my second year of tenure and it has remained indelibly in my innermost thoughts, always coming to the fore when I have mixed feelings about people and situations.

It came about because the status quo in the war zone remained a constant for many months, neither side making any progress, either diplomatically, or militarily, albeit skirmishes were sporadic and fortunately, fatalities minimal. It was however a farcical scenario, in that, whatever the allied forces carried out in their offensive guise, the enemy countered with similar tactics, but to a lesser degree and a tit for tat stalemate existed, which in military terms meant, several army regiments, the RAF, and spasmodically the Royal Navy, were kept busy by a very small cell of dissident tribesmen. Not a situation which was accepted easily by the authoritative council of elders, in other words the Military Commanders and those in high, local Parliamentary offices. The expense alone was prohibitive and the Government of the Protectorate could not afford to assist in the financial upkeep of a peace-keeping force, the magnitude of that which maintained in Aden. It was, however, the rightful duty of the British Government to protect its sovereign territories.

A very bizarre situation appeared to confound the allied forces and although it was seemingly an insignificant item, it caused much concern to the ground forces whose job it was to protect the accesses to the populated areas, in the Protectorate, which were, in essence, its very lifeline.

A few miles into the Radfan mountain range along a two mile strip of rough road, which was the only access to a very wide area of the enemy stronghold, in a period of two months, twelve military vehicles, ranging in size from personnel armored carriers, to jeeps, were destroyed, by land mines, with a heavy toll of life and equipment. This road was named the Dhala road, which lead far into the interior mountain region to the township of Dhala.

To maintain a constant presence in the area, would have demanded the deployment of two or three companies of soldiers on a continuous, rotational basis, which would not only deplete the infantry regiments engaged on internal security and other more pressing operations, but would put the soldiers in harms way, from marauding insurgents and sniper fire.

Ironically, and tragically, the mines were not confined only to causing the British soldiers to lose life and limb, but as the road was the main camel-trading route for the Arab merchants, many unsuspecting travelers were killed or maimed in the pursuit of their trade. This indiscriminate terrorist activity, did not differentiate between friend or foe and ultimately caused the merchants to discontinue their forays into the mountains, which in turn caused varying degrees of hardship to those who relied on the infrequent visits of the traders.

A decision was reached by the military, to eradicate this terrorist activity and the planning of such activity was confined to a need to know basis, until the day of its execution and was kept a very close secret.

On a very bright, warm, humid, November morning, just before nine o'clock, a large black Cadillac arrived at the SAR flight line, out of which, from the passenger compartment, emerged two, of what can only be described as the most beautiful garbed men, the like of which I had never seen.

Both men were of Arab origin, medium stature, with rugged weather-beaten complexions, suggesting that they were from an environment, which did not include air-conditioned offices and easy living. Their disposition was cool and menacing and their whole demeanor exuded professional confidence. The manner in which they arrived and the deference given to their presence, portrayed people of rare and unique significance.

Both men were dressed in the most magnificent costumes, easy flowing robes, made of what appeared to be a chiffon-like material, obviously suited for the task in hand. Contrasting, were the colors of both, one a deep lustrous pink, the other a bright turquoise. Splendid as the costumes were, they seemed entirely out of place in this drab, dusty, uninviting, desert landscape. In all of my recollections, I cannot forget the incongruity of those first fleeting moments of seeing those two warriors.

Apart from the magnificent garb, each man had crossed bandoleers of different caliber bullets strapped securely to their chests, both had an automatic pistol in a holster on their hips and an automatic, state of the art, rifle in hand and between them they carried an ammunition box in which was packed, the necessary munitions for their appointed task, which on reflection, could only be grenades and explosives of various types.

A second reserve helicopter had been prepared for this particular operation, the SAR equipment having been removed to keep the all-up weight as light as possible for reasons only the boss and his passengers were aware.

Without much ado, they climbed into the cabin of the helicopter and settled into their seats, their demeanor quiet and composed, it was, as if the whole operation were a daily routine akin to going to the office every morning, except that their office was a thousand square miles of desert and mountains.

The Flight Commander would fly the helicopter, ably assisted by a co-pilot instead of the navigator, the reason for which was evident, given the difficult nature of the operation.

Later it was learned that the two passengers were flown to a position several thousand feet up, adjacent to a very precipitous face of the mountain range, which faced the desert overlooking the Protectorate, where they were dropped off on a ledge, three thousand feet from the peak. This required a very skillful piece of flying as only one wheel of the helicopter could be actually placed on the ledge, whilst the other was suspended in space, the reason being the restriction placed on the helicopter by the close proximity of the rotor blades to the rock face.

Each passenger, along with his equipment, had to disembark by sliding down the right hand oleo leg, the ammunition box was then carefully handed to them by the co-pilot, while the pilot was holding the aircraft in a precarious hover, fighting the thermals and winds shift, which was no mean feat, but was another facet of the flying capabilities of Flight Lieutenant.C. Walton-Hadley.

Having made a safe exit from the helicopter the two men quickly disappeared into the rocky interior to carry out their assigned mission.

Ultimately, the mining of the Dhala road ceased, how this was accomplished, can only be surmised and remains a matter of conjecture, this situation maintained for at least, the remainder of my sojourn in Aden.

A job well done indeed and an outstanding example of allied forces cooperation in times of conflict and political upheaval.

Chapter Eleven

It was not too long after the Dhala road incident, that the Governor General of the Protectorate resigned from office, his frustration as to the way the British Government, in all their collective wisdom, had handled the whole middle east situation, precipitated this untimely and unfortunate move on his part.

His input as to how to handle the war effort in Aden, had been totally ignored by a very liberal minded Socialist Government and his military commanders, similarly, had their hands tied by the Chiefs of Staff, all of whom paid lip service to their civilian masters.

To be on the spot in a very volatile environment, to live a day to day existence in a hostile land, having a very comprehensive rapport with the local loyal Arab population, knowing the total picture of the political, economic and social situation and then to have calculated, objective, informed advice, summarily disregarded, by the faceless bureaucracy of Whitehall, was perhaps more than one dedicated individual should endure.

Within days of the Governor General's departure from Aden a new face appeared in the Governor's office, one appointee that would play the role of puppet to the Whitehall regime and a person with whom the military could not find common ground for their proposed actions and advice. This lead to a rather tenuous relationship between military and civilian authority, which in a wide area of conflict was not conducive to efficient, cordial operations, nor total acceptance of the status quo by all factions involved in the war effort.

Terrorism flourished in the ensuing months, both in the domestic and combat areas, the acts of barbarism perpetrated against the civilian populous was a never ending concern to the servicemen and their families, which precipitated an increased demand for tightened internal security measures, which in turn required more military personnel and had the perception of a snowball effect, which could only satisfy those who conducted their heinous acts, against women and children in the streets of Maala, Crater and Steamer Point, three of the local townships making up the Aden Peninsular.

Mosques were used for acts of subversion and I actually witnessed the throwing of a hand grenade from one, which was aimed at an army security patrol, fortunately, the perpetrator was not accurate in his endeavors and the grenade exploded harmlessly in a storm drain.

Perhaps the most vile of all the acts of terrorism, committed by those reactionary cowards, brought the fight to the lowest common denominator when they conducted outrageous atrocities against women and children, booby traps in school children's satchels, on school premises and buses, explosive devices in shops, banks and offices and anywhere people were likely to be working or relaxing, were only a few examples of the heinous, disgusting reign of torment and trauma exacted on the innocent, by the most contemptible of human beings.

Eventually my tour of duty came to an end in December of 1965, and I returned to the United Kingdom to an RAF Station in Oxfordshire, which was quite a contrast to my previous two years, but I managed to retain an interest in that part of the world which hitherto was my home, one which in the great scheme of things was little known by the majority of the world's population, but would in future years have a considerable effect on South Arabia.

South Yemen ultimately was annexed by the Russians and East Germans and all that was built up by the British was welcomed and used to create a communist authoritarian arena, which in effect, still exists to this day, much to the consternation of the local Arab population.

If an epilogue to this narrative, were to be written, it would probably reflect the best and worst of human behavior and would without fear of contradiction espouse the virtues of that which apparently evades us all, to respect and love our fellow man.

PREAMBLE

The readers of this narrative should appreciate the time line involved and the span of weeks, not months, over which this tale unfolds. Much is condensed, in a vain hope to capture the salient points of the story and much will probably be excluded in the interest of brevity.

The Beginning

I first met Gary Adams in the fall of 1989 during my tenure as General Manager with an aircraft engine overhaul and repair company, 'Paxford', situated in Miami, close to the international airport, which should have been running at a very nice profit, however, due to the frequent incursions by an inept, irresponsible owner, making truly outrageous business decisions, the bottom line was in all respects minimal, the law of 'diminishing returns' being enacted with academic perfection.

The owner, Edward Landry was an aging mid fifties, with a very pronounced affinity for the dramatic, especially when he had imbibed the previous evening with a modest quantity of Jack Daniels and a more than liberal libation the morning after. His outward congeniality was a facade, meant to portray an air of cordiality with business associates and friends alike and one of which all and sundry took full advantage. Many times, against all advice and counsel, customers, would request credit for services rendered and ultimately renege on the final request for payment. This would inevitably lead to a tightening of the company's financial accounts, until due restitution was made by the tardy customers. During this one year period, we always met payroll and more by luck than judgment kept reasonably balanced books.

Edward Landry, 'Ted' to his friends, for all of his lack of business acumen, had a very generous nature, his 'heart was in the right place', so the saying goes, which can be a veritable attribute but a deadly adversary should the ungodly choose to flout the very essence of the humane soul and it was thus that the following events transpired to the detriment of all that remains sacrosanct in the world of sentient human beings.

Ted called me one morning from his office "Keith, come and meet a friend of mine, he's in my office and wants to meet you". Naturally I assumed that the friend was a long standing colleague of Ted's who was visiting the region, as was the norm with his acquaintances, who frequently turned up for a free lunch, hoping to engender from him some business ideas, of which Ted had quite a repertoire, having, like myself, spent most of his life in aviation and made numerous associates, in many of the airlines and their affiliates.

Entering Ted's office I looked across the room to see a man rising from his chair to greet me and at that moment I had a vision that is indelibly imprinted on my mind and one which was to haunt me for the rest of my life, not in a frightening way but in a way that reminds me that I was gullible and naive to say the least where this man was concerned.

Ted said "Gary, meet Keith, my right hand man in this company", and continuing to doubly ensure the correct identification, which was not warranted, he said "Keith meet Gary Adams, a friend of mine and a business associate". At this juncture I should have known that a business associate to Ted would mean anyone from a gas station attendant to the CEO of Boeing and in all good conscience he could call on that type of corporate power, so it was a spontaneous judgment call when a business associate was introduced.

I shook Gary's hand and said it was good to meet him, all the time looking at his physical presence. He was at least six feet and three inches, with a very boyish round face, perched on top of his three hundred pound torso and although he appeared to have a corpulent gut he carried his weight very well. "Gary has been in the airline industry for many years and will probably do some high power business with us, in the near future," Ted interposed, "In fact he is working on an engine deal with Pan American at this moment, with any luck we can broker the engines for him ".

"Well Gary" I said, "Perhaps you can fill us in with a few details of your pending deal, so that we can source some potential customers".

Gary looked at me wistfully, reluctant to divulge too many secrets but I thought, if we were to be doing business in the short term we should have some mutual trust.

Gary sat down again in the one large arm chair that shared the office with Ted and spoke in a rather cultured indefinable North American voice, one which my short residence in the USA could not discern, but later to learn from Ted that it was an up-state New York accent. "I am currently negotiating with the Sales division of Pan American at JFK, to obtain all the relevant data prior to a physical inspection of the engines at a more convenient venue" Gary volunteered as if to pacify my piqued curiosity. "There are at least ten good engines available and a host of partially built ones of all types, including some large fans worth several million on the open market and more on some select foreign markets". This was good news for all of us but I was reticent in my acceptance of how all this hardware was available and we in the business were not aware of such a potential bonanza, the' bush telegraph' being somewhat alive and well in our industry and covered the aviation world spectrum, hence my skepticism.

I took my leave of Gary and Ted, on the pretext that I had some pressing work assignments to finish up, which was not too far from the truth, but I wanted to authenticate the claims that Gary had brought to us and as with the more seasoned veterans of this aviation industry, I had numerous colleagues who could obtain the information which I would require to carry on with the business of seeking buyers for the supposed glut of spare aircraft engines which were about to flood the market.

I reflected on the brief meeting with Ted and Gary and wondered from what pedigree Gary came and resolved to question Ted on the subject at the earliest opportunity. In most legal businesses it is prudent to know with whom you are dealing and in the interests of all of ones associates and for the financial health of your enterprise, knowing your friends and adversaries is a logical step in the dealings and negotiations which are a finite part of the business world.

The Profile

Ted was out of the office the following day, so I had time to ruminate on the subject of Gary Adams. Who was he?, where did he come from?, how was he connected in this rather esoteric business?, how did he come by such information?, which should have been general knowledge in our business as it was a deal which could net the brokers substantial returns, by substantial, I mean millions of dollars. Aircraft engines by their very definition are very expensive, highly technical, precision, pieces of machinery and in many instances, are diligently sought after by commercial airlines and other aircraft operators located worldwide and indeed at times create a competitive bidding process between interested factions.

Things did not add up too easily and I made a few cursory discreet telephone calls to my friends and colleagues around the country, intentionally not giving away any commercial information which could be used to usurp the pending deal between Gary and his benefactors, as this was an industry and a city where crooked deals and subversive liaisons were prevalent.

My first inquiries, which were through personal acquaintances knew nothing of one Gary Adams, nor had any of my associates ever heard of him, which was not in itself significant, however, no one had heard of the batch of engines that were supposedly for sale, nor where they would possibly originate, as most people in the industry had many sources of information and could track a potential deal within hours of an inquiry, after which it would be the survival of the most affluent and the corporate companies with the influence in circles where only the well connected could deal and ultimately prosper, by finalizing a deal, the maxim of "it's not what you know but who you know," is, in all walks of life, the fateful unfortunate truth.

I decided not to dwell on the how's, why's and when's of my thought provoking meeting with Gary Adams, after all, we would be partial beneficiaries of any deal consummated between Gary and his business associates.

Ted came into office the following Monday, after his business trip which was supposedly a meeting with some engine dealers who presumably had something to offer us, however I did not press the issue as I wanted to keep Ted's mind on the subject of Gary.

"Good morning Ted", I said walking into his office, "Before we get down to the business of last week's reports, I want to ask you what Gary Adams has to contribute to our enterprise", Ted looked up from his daily paper, which was a morning reading ritual with him, if it were not for coffee, cigarettes and the morning paper, life, to him, would not have much meaning and perhaps my intrusion with a seemingly inconsequential inquiry, was not received in the best possible way.

I sat down across the desk from him and waited until his conscience allowed him to look up from his newspaper. "What was it you wanted to talk to me about, that couldn't wait ", Ted said brusquely, "I need peace and quiet on Monday mornings, especially after a hard weekend driving around Florida". I gathered from that piece of rhetoric that his wife was in town badgering him to find more suitable semi-permanent accommodation, instead of living in the local tenement suites, on a month to month basis, which was convenient for a month to month bachelor, but in no way coincides with the feminine idealism which permeates every corridor of the male psyche. Ted had moved up from Texas to fulfill a contractual requirement, but his wife Doris had no intention of moving away from her beloved San Antonio.

"Where did you meet Gary Adams and how did you manage to persuade him to divulge his business plans to you"

"He's a friend of one of my colleagues from my previous employers and he vouches for him one hundred per cent" Ted said rather pompously, the implication being that my question was out of place, however, I intended to protect the company from any untoward difficulties which could easily accrue from an alliance bent on maximizing profits for the business partner, irrespective of how subjective Ted's reasons were.

"Well Ted let's be careful and find out more about the deal and assure ourselves that there is a reasonable chance of us making an acceptable profit".

"There wont be any trouble, he's well known in the industry and he used to Fly Jumbo Jets (Boeing 747 aircraft) for Pan Am and has international contacts which we can make use of'" little did I know at that time how well connected his contacts were and how they fitted into the business and commercial world and with what accreditation.

"He told you he was a pilot with Pan American?" I said

"Yes and he had to stop flying for medical reasons".

"Well that sounds reasonable, however, for him to move into the big commercial world of buying and selling aircraft engines and spare parts, he must be well connected". I said with a hint of sarcasm.

Ted looked at me knowingly and with a wry smile said "If the deal is as big as Gary says it is, then we will be in for a very healthy commission".

I could tell that he was in no mood to converse on any subject, let alone discuss any subject which might bring his decision-making into question, so I decided to go to my office and do some work which might gain us some revenue, which after all, is what we were employed to do.

Thinking about the conversation between Ted and myself, made me think of all the misconceptions and inevitable graft that exists in the aviation industry and Miami was the center of most of the criminal activity connected with the scams and nefarious so-called business dealings associated with the South American connection, which was notorious for much suspected transfer of contraband, of every description into and out of the United States. Aviation was and is the medium by which those transactions are made possible.

From my first encounter with Gary, cursory as it was, my intuitive senses were piqued and my instinctive enquiring engineering mind was stimulated to a point that I knew I must inevitably engage Gary in conversation, putting to rest, or otherwise, the nagging concerns I had about the way in which this corpulent entity had entered my business life, most of which were, at that time, of a general nature, fairly vague, but given the portents of what could become a potential financial disaster if the company were to subsidize a venture, then fail to capitalize on it, my employment and that of the employees would be of very little academic interest.

To root out the basis of Gary's involvement, I had to conceive an approach which would ultimately determine a positive analysis of the situation and resolve in my mind the angles of his business agenda, my whole intent to forestall any potential damage to our business, which in the existing economic climate, could be catastrophic.

My reticence to ask outright poignant questions, was borne out of an uncertainty as to how genuine Gary may be and to spoil a potential business arrangement, by crass stupidity, was not a viable option at that point in time. Subtlety had not always been my greatest ally, but I inwardly vowed to be cautious in my attempt at my objective sleuthing.

My chance came one Monday morning when Ted was in transit from his home in Texas, returning to Florida, having just spent a long weekend with his family, as was his monthly sojourn, one which was dictated by his ever-loving wife, long suffering as she was, with Ted traveling the globe during the course of his employment contracts,

Gary came to the reception desk and I was informed of his arrival by Sally, the receptionist, secretary, coffee maker and general factotum, who was a very dedicated and organized person, which was good for the operation, in the light of Ted's inability to pursue any given topic to its ultimate conclusion. More of that, at a later time.

I invited Gary into my office on the pretext that I was expecting an overseas call, which in itself was not a lie as I was in fact waiting for some feedback from my former aviation colleagues in England, on my current dilemma, which for obvious reasons I did not divulge to Gary.

Gary sat in the only chair that would contain his formidable bulk and I asked Sally to bring some coffee and a cup of tea for me, with milk incidentally, which is the acceptable way to drink hot tea and maintain a regimented protocol of British derivation. Unfortunately the niceties of formal etiquette were lost on the less-informed of the coffee drinking fraternity, not wasted, however, as my enjoyment of the beverage outweighed any conceived ignorance by my peers, of a bygone heritage.

We chatted about many incidental and mostly boring subjects, until I had a chance to broach the matter of his aviation and business experience, which came in a not-too-subtle way when the conversation bordered on the business opportunities available in the aviation industry

"How did you make the transition from flying to the commercial business world" I asked in a rather nonchalant manner."It wasn't easy and flying became an obligatory occupation which was increasingly demanding on my personal life, with many irregular hours, coupled with the countless inconsistencies in the company's policies, which was beginning to affect my health, so I made the decision to opt out while I was young enough to start something new". Gary was probably in his mid forties, so it was a feasible explanation and I did not pursue the matter.

"Did your aviation experience influence your decision as to your choice of business enterprises"? .I countered.

"Yes in a manner of speaking, the noticeable trend of the commercial aviation world of aircraft accessories, giving rise to more than acceptable profits, certainly influenced my decision".

"Did your former career as a commercial pilot help you to make business contacts,?

"Not until I realized that many of my former colleagues were also dabbling in the aircraft spare parts business." he said in a laconic tone.

I tried not to be too specific in my inquisition, so I decided to explore another avenue, one which could possibly enlighten me as to the professional abilities of this big man, at the same time giving him a chance to recount his flying prowess, which most pilots tend to do whenever the situation presents itself, indicative of course, of the inflated, egotistical opinion most pilots have of themselves.

"I'll bet you got a kick out of flying the big ships." I said, trying to sound flippant and friendly, one aviation professional to the other, I was naturally referring to the Jumbo Jets specifically, the Boeing 747 aircraft which he had purported to have flown with Pan American Airways as captain and pilot in command. "It was always a thrill to know that you had control of such a behemoth, with the constant reminder that four hundred people were relying on you to safely bring them to their chosen destination." He said with an air of superiority. I knew at that point I could squeeze the remainder of his delusions of grandeur from his self-effacing egotistical posturing. For the next half an hour I fed his ego with general questions on flying and the places of interest, which he supposedly had flown to in his career as an aviator. At that point, I thrust at him a technical question, which any pilot of any commercial aircraft would know, without hesitation.

"The flight system on the Boeing 747 is a triplex fail passive system isn't it?" I posed the question more as a query for my own interest, but knowing the answer was the ace in the hole for me. He hesitated for several second before answering.

"Yes it has a twice redundant fail safe system, which is totally state of the art technology."

A good answer I thought, however, completely incorrect, but to give him the benefit of the doubt, owing to the fact that his memory may have clouded somewhat in the intervening period of his inactive flying months-years-days, whatever the case, I pressed on with another pertinent question, one which would completely define his flying knowledge or otherwise render it superfluous.

"I suppose all the information for en-rout navigation flying is pre-programmed on discs and entered before flight by the flight crew."

Gary became rather quiet as he realized this line of questioning may inevitably cost him his pre-qualified integrity with our company, which Ted had afforded him, one which could subsequently flaw his credibility with any future business dealings, so his tardy reply was evasively vague, to say the least and not in any way, shape, or form definitive.

"I cannot answer that with any accuracy as subsequent modifications to the electronic systems, since my flying days, on the Boeings may have installed various innovative technology, including the one you have suggested." He replied guardedly.

To refer to modern commercial aircraft flight systems as 'electronic systems' instead of 'avionics systems' as any person conversant with the term would know, completely and decisively made my analysis of his aviation knowledge a negative. So then, where was he from? What credibility did he have in our business? , how did he come by the business information which he alluded to and was it from credible sources?. Many questions formed in my mind and I resigned myself to try and resolve some of them in the near future, I did however give him the benefit of the doubt for his technical lapses, as it was just possible that he was not current with the most innovative aviation technology.

I pondered the discussion which I had entered into with Gary and found myself not liking the way in which I had tried to elicit information from a total stranger who for all the world was a genuine participant in the future of our business association and if he were as disingenuous as I believed him to be, he would not mention our conversation to Ted, not wanting to sow the seeds of doubt in the minds of those who would ultimately be his benefactors in whatever plans he had laid for his business ventures.

Thus I played the waiting game to hear any misgivings from my associates, in the unlikely event that Gary queried my conversation with one or all of my colleagues. No such event was evident in the next few days and I continued to make mental points for my cerebral dossier of one Gary Adams.

Thinking to myself, that many items which I had posed as probable reasons why Gary Adams was not what he said he was, prompted me to think of my airline experience and a question arose as to how any airline pilot, especially the size of Gary, could undergo an annual physical and pass without a hitch. On reflection, all pilots of my acquaintance were fairly fit, not obese and fairly active, so how did Gary's size weigh against him at his annual visit to the flight surgeon?. Obviously, there had to be a reason for his continued presence on the flight deck, if indeed his story was true and this particular subject was not one that could be approached directly, as personal problems were not part of the business scene, and must be avoided at all costs if professional harmony and mutual courtesy maintain in such a small unit as in our domain.

Most reputable airlines have very stringent codes, whereby its employees are tested for proficient technical and physical abilities at predetermined intervals and those whose work areas are involved directly with aircraft, such as flight operations and maintenance, which are particularly scrutinized for the obvious hearing and seeing impairment. For this reason alone I suspected that Gary had hidden agendas.

My concerns for the fiscal well being of the company led me to pursue avenues other than the personal front and I continued to be as subtle as my demeanor allowed to elicit more information concerning the proposed deals made by Gary.

The Pan American deal seemed to founder in the ensuing days and I did not press the issue with Ted, but took another tack which could possibly lead to my enlightenment on potential business accounts.

"Ted, what deals do we have cooking at the moment" I said, eyeing the various paperwork on his desk, which was in total disarray, but par for the course, as tidiness was not next to Godliness in Ted's world.

"Gary has another deal pending with Lufthansa in Hamburg. There are several engines available and we are working a deal with Wally Grant to put the engine accessory units through his shop and split the engines for the discs and burner cans and any other internal components which have acceptable time left to run".

"Good" I replied "Perhaps we can get some genuine parts from those engines, How many did you say were available?".

"At least ten, perhaps more, but Gary is trying to get the disc and core paperwork from them, so that we can assess the work scopes required to rebuild some engines and disassemble those which we know will not have sufficient hours and cycles left to rebuild"

"When you receive the data, let me have a look at the disc sheets and we can work through the times and cycles and compile a matrix which will give us a better indication of which ones to use and where" I said, hoping that I did not get an argument as to whom should assess the documentation.

"OK will do" Ted said, perhaps hoping that I would not ruffle any feathers unduly if I had the control of the quite complex documentation. "In fact I have other business to attend to and Gary and I will be moving around somewhat in the next few days, but I will keep you posted".

I walked out of the office and back to mine thinking that perhaps something may come of the German deal, which would be lucrative to say the least and may put my mind to rest especially if our bank account were to increase substantially.

The Associates

Wally Grant had what is known as an Accessory Shop, in Miami, which meant he was duly authorized by the Federal Aviation Administration to overhaul and repair aircraft components, and he specialized in engine accessory units, such as constant speed drives (CSD) integrated drive generators (IDG) and many smaller fuel and hydraulic components. His business was successful and his business ethic impeccable and thus his reputation spread and his business thrived accordingly.

To say that Wally Grant was a gentleman in all respects, is to epitomize his way of life and disseminate him from the odorous aviation community of Miami .He was gracious to a fault and unlike Ted and his counterparts, did not use expletives nor discriminatory gestures to make a point of conversation. His demeanor was a joy to behold and in my extensive worldly experience I considered it refreshing to converse with him on any subject without recourse to extraneous innuendo and self-indulgent invective.

Perhaps it was his previous professional life that gave rise to his demeanor, I learned from those who had known him for a long period of time that he was a professional ballet teacher and as he grew older and less supple in mind and body, he moved into a completely different environment, which he adjusted to admirably and as with his former vocation he succeeded where many had failed.

As part of the proposed deal with Lufthansa, Wally would take the engine accessory units, which would be removed on receipt of the engines and perform the necessary maintenance on them in his work shops, the work to be accomplished would be assessed when all historical records of the components were known and evaluated, a job which would take an experienced technician, a good deal of time, however, knowing the thoroughness of the Lufthansa maintenance and records department, the job should flow easily.

I was unaware, until some days later that Gary Adams had made a deal with Wally Grant, whereby Wally would put up the initial deposit for the engines of one hundred and fifty thousand US dollars, which he would recuperate when the sale of the accessory units finally took place. Not only did Wally put up the initial deposit he volunteered to carry the work load and the expense thereof, until such time as the accessory units were sold, a magnanimous gesture for someone who did not have one shred of evidence that the deal would be consummated and manifested, other than the word of his good friend Ted Landry, who in such diverse times would vouch for anyone he thought might be a genuine source of revenue, a tribute to his good hearted character, but not to his business acumen.

The folly of this deal was, no one questioned Gary as to why he did not personally fund the initial deposit, another element of his persuasive ability, which apparently went unnoticed by his peers and business associates, or was not broached to him directly, but obviously resonated around Ted's attestation of Gary's worth as a business associate. Gary obviously made the deal with

Wally, which sounded very attractive with the promises of high percentage returns on his investment, which in all respects was a very reasonable expectation, given the potential quality of the components concerned. Large deals involving very large sums of money, such as the one purported to be in the melting pot, of necessity, can be of a very protracted nature, this was a facet of all the proposed deals Gary had brought to the table and in retrospect took a very disciplined mind to plan and execute several deals concurrently with such definitive precision, culminating in a very lucrative return on his investment.

At fairly regular intervals, Gary had a visitor, who for all intents and purposes was his benefactor, or it was that all outward indications led one to believe that it was the case.

Peter or 'Pete' as he wanted to be called, was a lanky Texan, who purported to have some business affiliations to the oil companies in Houston and Galveston. He appeared to be a very personable character and was at ease with everyone, his southern drawl coupled with a very outward personality endeared him to my colleagues and business associates alike.

Pete was obviously independently wealthy, well dressed, even in jeans and high-heeled boots, expensively tailored shirts and hair well groomed, he personified the true image of a Texas gentleman.

If the truth were to be known, and a consensus taken amongst my business associates, Pete gave Gary the credibility, which, I considered was patently lacking and in my estimation Gary's persona moved up a notch on my esteem gage.

Pete's visits were not more than a day or two at a time and mostly spent in the company of Gary, supposedly discussing business affairs and as Ted would have me believe, their confidential meeting times were evidently spent in the bar of the hotel where both Gary and Pete were guests. Gary incidentally, preferred the more luxurious accommodations found at Miami Beach and supposedly paying the exorbitant rates for the privilege. Little did I know at the time what the financial arrangements were for his tenure.

Jim and Roland were co-owners of an aircraft engine overhaul shop, namely 'B and B engines Inc' conveniently located two blocks away form our company offices and were a very successful partnership, both having been in the profession for many years and one complimented the other, Jim controlling the practical aspect of the overhaul shop and Roland the financial and sales side of the operation. Both were kind, generous, knowledgeable and always ready for a challenge, which Ted invariably presented them, which at this particular time, was in the guise of Gary Adams.

It did not take a Professor of Psychology to deduce that another deal had been struck, with the able assistance of Ted, between Gary Adams and the partnership. All seemed well and all parties were, for all outward appearances, satisfied with the arrangements, whereby the overhaul shop would potentially receive all the dismantled engines and rebuild those which could be salvaged and made whole, after which they could be sold, with a sizeable spares package created from those parts which were not used during the rebuilds, for a really substantial amount of money, which would then be divided among the various factions. This sounded fair and equitable, depending upon who made the allocation of percentages and it was another fairly reasonable guess, who that person would be.

My doubts about the viability of the proposed alliances seemed to wilt somewhat in the light of the deals that were 'consummated' whether documented or verbal and the number of people involved, surely it was safe to assume, that nothing shady would transpire, too many known players, all of whom were reputable solid professional businessmen.

Intelligence

Steve Cannon was a long standing friend of mine from the United Kingdom and had been in the aviation industry almost as long as myself and as the occasion demanded I talked with him at length on matters various and the aviation world in particular. He was a good source of information and a very knowledgeable person, discreet to a fault with a very detailed memory. Information was a two-way street and I would pass along anything I thought might interest him professionally and he would reciprocate. Nothing that passed between us could be construed as a conflict of interests, so our conversations, although mostly topical, were stimulating for both of us as we could impart totally different aspects of a mutual occupation, him from the UK and European point of view and me from that of The United States.

A conversation which I had with Steve in the early February of that year, later came to haunt me and in retrospect made me feel sad and morose, after my obvious lame attempts to portray my misgivings on certain current aircraft engine deals, which at that time had absolutely nothing to do with Steve Cannon.

"Hi Steve" I said waiting for his usual repartee.

"Oh!! So you have found time to call me, have you" he replied, in his usual sardonic manner.

"Yes, and I apologize for not having called you sooner,

but as usual my excuse is 'pressure of work' as always".

"Well" he said "Better late than never, What's new in your world?."

"Do me a favor" I said." See if you can find out if Lufthansa is selling a bunch of Pratt and Whitney JT8 and JT9 engines and what terms are they offering, as I have heard that a deal is in the pipeline and we as a company may get involved".

"I haven't heard any whispers of anything from the Continent, but I will do my due diligence and let you know, but don't hold your breath, it wont be for a week or so" he said.

"OK with me Steve, however, if there is any inkling that a deal exists, call me ASAP, will you."

For the better part of another hour we conversed on other matters, most of which would be considered trivia in a world where extraneous chit chat had no credence. We did however enjoy the reminiscence of our early days when we were both employed at the same facility in England.

At no time did I divulge the originator of the potential deals with Lufthansa, however, I knew that if there were an authentic contract issued by the airline for the sale of engines, Steve would find out the details and I would act accordingly. My fervent hope for the sake of all parties was that the deal was genuine and could be a money-maker, which for my company would give a more stable financial platform for future business, than the one which currently existed.

Another Associate

Irvin Shoemaker, was introduced into the consortium by Ted Landry and was purported to be a long standing friend oh his from Austin, Texas. Having previously alluded to Ted's understanding of what constituted a long standing friend. I am not to this day, entirely sure of the personal connections between the two, suffice to say Irvin became an integral player in the events yet to unfold.

Irvin was a renaissance man, having a finger in many and varied businesses, which by all outward appearances made him a good living. His business trips took him all over the USA and travel was made easy and simple due his ownership of a twin-engine Jetstar aircraft which he prized above all other worldly possessions.

I met him on several occasions and found him to have a very solid personality, outgoing and certainly a logical thinker, with very strict ideals, which to his credit he tried to live up to.

Apart from his skills as a pilot he was an adept gunsmith and on reflection this was probably the catalyst, which endeared him to Ted, as both were avid gun lovers and obviously enjoyed the rapport each had with the other.

Charisma is a word I seldom use, mainly because it is a nebulous word which does not define one given trait in a person, it is a mélange of conglomeration and innuendo which leaves imagination a high degree of latitude to make up any characteristic, one chooses to apply to any given person, whether they are a pop idol, a prominent political figure or a prolific athlete.

Gary Adams had the innate ability to coerce, persuade, engender, or I could use any of the descriptive superlatives which might accurately describe his demeanor, but truthfully, if charisma encompassed them all, it would probably be as indicative of his true self as any other adjective one could conjure up, even given the time and the thought processes so to do.

Practicalities

At the outset of Ted's liaison with Gary, of necessity, means of communication, projected contract dates, timetables for negotiations, meetings with all relevant parties, had to be arranged and it was incumbent upon Ted to coordinate and finance these events, Why? Because Ted wanted to be the focal point of all business dealings, after all it was *he* who had persuaded Gary to join the business venture and all other interested parties seemingly took a back seat and went with the tide. My innermost thoughts imagined everyone singing "For he's a jolly good fellow" but sanity regained a firm grip on my levity, when I reflected the portents of what the outcome of all this bonhomie might be, which again did nothing for my now dormant ego.

To say that my business day was centered around our normal business commitments, such as ordering spare parts for customers engines which were already in house, or ensuring the documentation for work in progress was OK and the work force was performing well and organizing shift staffing for the projected work load, detracted somewhat from the euphoric atmosphere which pervaded the company, in the light of the proposed, supposed, upcoming bonanza, orchestrated by Ted and Gary. I tried to remain aloof, but nagging thoughts reared their ugly heads, every time I turned my mind to Gary Adams.

Doubts

Encountering Ted on his way to lunch one morning, I enquired as to how the deals were progressing. "As good as I had expected" he said, somewhat sullenly, which could have meant anything, but my translation of his mood did not auger well, things did not appear to be working out too well, which might have been the beginning of a minor dissention in the on-going contract negotiations. Not knowing the details controlling his mood, I continued on my way to the shop to arrange some extra space for some incoming work. I later found out the reason for his demeanor and although a minor infraction had arisen, it did not appear at the time to be insurmountable.

At the outset of the business arrangement with Gary, it was agreed by Ted that all communication equipment would be provided by our company, which would be part of the recompense when engines and parts sales came to fruition, thus, although at the time cellular phones were in their infancy and rather cumbersome, both Ted and Gary were endowed with one each. Initial expenditure came as a shock to Ted but his agreement with Gary, albeit verbal, was solid and a matter of 'my word is my bond' on Ted's part, maintained and continued for the length of their liaison.

All hotel bills for Gary at the lavish Miami Beach resort were another contentious issue and again were paid for by the company with a similar understanding to that of the cellular phones deal. I was afraid that at any given time in the near future the liquidity of the company would be at risk, hence again I inquired of Ted; "I can see we are having a shortfall in our cash flow" I said, approaching Ted in his cigarette smoke-filled office. "Don't worry about that." He said. "Once the first engine comes through we will recuperate all initial expenditure, plus a healthy profit".

At this point I countered, "When do you expect this to happen, as you know we are limited to what we can spend monthly as the annual budget dictates and at this moment in time we are in the "Red".

"How can we be in the "Red?" he said, "Our income from direct sales and parts are giving us a good return on our investment and with our normal work load we must be financially solvent".

My patience at this point was running thin and my reply to his rather uninformed remark was "Well perhaps we had better ask our accountant to reconcile the books, perhaps then you will understand the significance of my statement which was not made to ruin your day, but to make you aware of the current situation".

With that said, I exited the office and went about my daily duties, knowing full well that Ted would ruminate on my comments and maybe take some positive remedial action. My thoughts would not allow me the pleasure of an instinctive sarcastic reaction, so I went about my business, hoping to assuage my negative thoughts, by indulging myself in some constructive and hopefully profitable work, as my work ethic seemed to be taking a down turn, every time I spoke with Ted, especially when the subject angled towards Gary..

I tried to sum up the current situation, which bothered me more than a little. We had to meet the weekly payroll for the direct employees and I was hoping that our debtors would pay their accounts on time and thus maintain enough surplus for the extraneous spending which was happening on a daily basis at an increasing rate. I would have to do some calling to our customers to expedite any early payments, as most of our customers were on a sixty day payment plan and fortunately our customer data base was extremely good and I knew that I would get a positive reaction from a high percentage of them.

My summation was faltering somewhat, when I started to itemize the negative spending which was taking place and being cumulative in nature, figures started to jump out of my computer screen with alarming regularity.

Cellular phones, escalating office phone bills, Miami Beach hotel accommodation, travel (at the moment within the USA), diminishing petty cash, automobile gas bills (all 'Paxford' credit cards) lunches and dinners, entertainment (for whatever occasion presented itself) and so on. *Please* let these proposed engine deals be a reality or else my job and those of our employees would be in jeopardy.

To further complicate matters, as the tale eventually unfolded, Ted had guaranteed the reimbursement to our 'partners', if during the course of the seemingly protracted efforts at negotiations with Lufthansa, they incurred expenses out of their normal budgeted range. A real magnanimous offer.

Travel

It was around the middle of February when travel plans suddenly became an important issue, mainly because the whole engine deal evolved around potential customers wanting the restored engines and parts packages, it therefore became a priority to meet with the interested parties, 'face to face', according to Ted. This arrangement involved extensive travel within the continental USA, as many of the potential customers were in remote parts of country.

At this point in time, it must be germane to mention that nobody, including Ted and I suspected Gary had not seen any tangible or documentary evidence of the supposed aircraft engines. Not a wise business situation in which to find oneself and I tried my uttermost to reconcile my doubting conscience, by trying to rationalize my fears in the hope that Ted was aware of all the pitfalls which could materialize at any given moment. How naive can I be? with all that was overtly happening. Saints preserve me!.

Facilitating the travel plans, was of course the domain of Ted and Gary and included at least a week away from the office and of necessity, required a very intricate itinerary, owing to the vast distances involved and the time changes, hotel reservations etc., which was time-consuming and I left that privilege to Ted and Gary, after all they were the beneficiaries of this business jaunt, or should I say junket. I had to keep the firm as solvent as possible by maintaining a rigid disciplined attitude to my duties, which was difficult with all the extraneous activity buzzing around me.

Later as the events unfolded, with the input from all of the factions involved in the deals which were germane to the overall game plans, I learned that Irvin Shoemaker was coerced, or charmed, as the case maybe, by our dynamic duo, to be party to the travel arrangements, by flying the entourage to the various parts of the country to be visited, again with the verbal agreement that all expenses would be paid by Ted and Gary at some more opportune time in the future, which was not too well defined, these expenses to include but not limited to, fuel, landing fees, ad hoc maintenance en route and any incidentals which can occur with any aircraft operation.

Hotel accommodation, food, refreshments and sundries would be paid by credit cards, the owners of which were Ted, Jim, Roland and Irvin. Of course this was Gary's deal and his persuasive powers had inculcated, with positive and very viable reasoning, that there would be much to gain from the tour and the recompense would be gratifying to say the least, giving the participants a very healthy gratuity. Wally Grant was the only unwitting party from the business group who would not travel with the others, but he had already contributed to the coffers by the infusion of one hundred and fifty thousand dollars.

How naïve! How gullible! that, intelligent, rational human beings, would be led into a series of potential fraudulent transactions without the inkling of whether the dealings were real and legal, having themselves been in the industry for many years and knowing the 'nature of the beast', especially in the Miami area.No perception of the aircraft engines, no documentary evidence of such, no direct conversation with those who were purported to own the said engines, nothing to substantiate that a deal was real, except the tenuous proclamations of Gary Adams. Was I really a willing pawn in this complex game of financial chess?, the answer was a resounding affirmative!.

Money is said to be the 'root of all evil', however the philosophers honed the phrase to read 'the love of money is the root of all evil' and a more apt expression could not be more fitting for the story at hand. 'Greed' has always been the source of conflicts from time immemorial, there never seems to be a mutual understanding when money, property or power are concerned. In many cases where litigants contest their supposed rights, the stronger of the parties will ultimately survive, depending upon the amounts of monies spent on the legal representation, however, when a confidence trickster absconds with his' ill gotten gains' there seems be little effective recourse for the victims of such impropriety, even if the perpetrator is apprehended and ultimately incarcerated, whatever is lost, remains lost.

More Improprieties

It was at this juncture that I was tempted to call my friend Steve Cannon in England, to ascertain the state of the aviation industry in Europe and in particular the supposed engine transaction that was about to unfold in Hamburg, which would obviously produce this lucrative windfall for everyone involved in the USA.

I was in a cynical mood when I called Steve and he rarely missed my moods, even though I would try to hide my feelings as much as possible and my dialogue with him did not engender any sympathy on his part for my deep concern for the current situation in the USA.

"Hi Steve", I said. What's the good news from England today."

"Good news is what you expect, bad news is what I have for you, so don't interrupt me before I have finished my Litany" he said in a rather loud and pompous manner.

"If it's all that bad perhaps you will allow me the consummate pleasure of not having to listen to a protracted dialogue and be succinct and clear, so that I can assimilate the facts and not have the clutter that normally accompanies your comments". My tone very argumentative but not in any way pernicious, which I know he accepted as my characteristic personal banter.

Steve always gave as good as he got and his retort to my comments was short and very succinct. "In that case I will keep you guessing and be very verbose, which I know you will appreciate in your dire anxiety to discover my findings."

"Thanks Steve." I said, hoping he would detect my relaxed tone.

"Don't mention it old boy, I like the fact that you await my pleasure occasionally." he said. I could imagine his pleasure as he made his point by laughing in his inimitable way.

"OK" Steve said. "I have gleaned as much information as I could from various sources, including an associate of mine in Munich, who has inside information from a source in Hamburg with close ties to Lufthansa. I asked about the impending deal for the engine sales and he denied any deal existed. Not to be out done I called another contact in Berlin and he confirmed the previous statement".

"Could your sources have personal conflicts of interests and are trying to convince you that a deal does not exist at the same time hoping to ingratiate themselves with Lufthansa and make a deal of their own" I said, hoping that he would not think that I was impugning their professional integrity, which after some thought, was what it sounded like and I immediately reprimanded myself, bur did not voice my inward apologies.

"Emphatically No!!" he responded, with a distinct edge in his voice. "Neither one has the inclination nor the financial backing to indulge themselves in any sort of back-door deals, furthermore I have known these chaps for many years and trust them implicitly". This said, I immediately mentally withdrew my follow up questions, which would have queried further the authenticity of Steve's remarks, instead I changed the subject matter as not to offend Steve any more than I had obviously done, by my fatuous remarks.

"Have you ever been contacted by a character calling himself Gary Adams", I said. "He is an associate of my colleagues here in the States, and purports to have a plethora of business contacts all over the world".

"No I can't say that I can recall the name" he replied, abruptly, but nevertheless I considered it truthful even though his tone was somewhat disquieting.

The remainder of the conversation alluded to more personal subjects and after another half an hour I said goodbye and turned my attention to my daily tasks.

From time to time with the limited conversations which I had with Gary, he would enquire about my life in England and in an unobtrusive way, on reflection, probably gleaned quite a bit of information from me, which at the time did not unduly worry me, it was later in the year that I learned that his devious file-cabinet mind had digested all that was said between us and I like an unwitting litigant, completing an unofficial question-naire, finally realized that this information could be used against me and my colleagues for the benefit of some illicit and fraudulent deals, which I knew could possible happen, given my new found knowledge concerning the disingenuous nature of Gary's propositions and probable unlikely deals with Lufthansa Airlines.

During the course of the fact finding mission of Ted, Gary and associates, which was one day short of a week, including travel time, I subsequently learned that much money was spent in the form of the credit cards, all except Gary, proffering the required fees and taxes, even to the ridiculous situation of Irvin paying for all the required fuel for his aircraft, which ran into the thousands of dollars, the exact total was never shared with me, and I did not broach the subject, even at a later date as temperaments were running high and volatile.

It transpired that the trip was a success and many prospective customers were interested in the potential offerings of the Lufthansa engines. This boded well for the whole party and left all involved with a more contented feeling about Gary and his impending deals. My inner-most thoughts were of imminent disaster.

The following day I talked with Ted concerning the day to day business, mentioning my recent conversation with Steve in England, but due to the fact that he was in a hurry to get away from the office, virtually ignoring my obvious innuendo, I decided to postpone the inevitable for a more opportune time, but was steadfast in my resolve to further pursue the subject.

His reason for such a speedy departure from the office was due to the imminent arrival from the United Kingdom of Gary's girl friends, two to be exact, they would be guests of the company at the same hotel on Miami Beach as Gary's tenure. Expense appeared to be no object and this time my naivety led me to believe that at least Gary would contribute some financial offering, as would any normal person who entertains friends or colleagues. This was not the case, how could I be so wrong ?.

It seemed that all impending deals were shelved for a few days while Gary played and Ted went along for the food and drinks. I was invited to one evening function, which I gracefully declined, as it would as always with Ted, degenerate into an alcoholic, miasmic, meaningless event which all would suffer from, the following day.

It was during this hiatus that another event unfolded, which again was learned about in retrospect, one that was seemingly insignificant in the scheme of things, but certainly effected my personal situation.

I had in the previous year invested in a travel agency in Fort Lauderdale, which was managed by a Jamaican lady, who at the time was holding her own in the very competitive world of travel, so I did not interfere in the day to day running of the agency, but looked in occasionally when I had the time and inclination or when business decisions had to be made which would effect the finances of the enterprise directly.

One day in January of that year, the exact date and day was academic, Gary entered the premises during the normal working hours of the agency and presented himself as a very good friend and colleague of mine and that I had given him express permission to use my office and particularly the telephone.

This of course was not true, but the lady in question did not advise me of this happening and it was some months until I learned of the repercussions of this incursion, when I was auditing the facility and found to my chagrin that many long distance and international calls had been made to the tune of two thousand dollars. Needless to say I immediately challenged the Manager who unwittingly allowed this vagary to occur, but as with all things involved with Gary Adams, his undeniable charm had won the day and as the saying goes "suckered me".

The Showdown

I do not know who coined the phrase, "Sufficient unto the day is the evil thereof", but this seemed to fit the whole scenario of that period in my life when Gary Adams came to Miami in an aura of confident yet cordial manner, inviting himself into a very gullible array of people, who, although not highly attuned to the skullduggery of the nefarious flim-flam men, sought to indulge a fellow human being in a legitimate business relationship, which ultimate went awry.

Arbitrarily, one could argue that 'All is Fair in Love and War', but is it? Armed with the knowledge that an entity could possibly be endowed with certain inalienable gifts, that used in a specific way, could turn an otherwise perfect situation into utter chaos, belies the accepted principle that all men are created equal.

Arguably, it could be said that Ted Landry and his business associates consciously intended to use Gary Adams for the sole purpose of making a quick profit, given that they understood the ramifications of the potential deals not materializing, using their undeniable expertise in their given professions. One salient yet important facet, which did not enter the equation, was the 'nature of the beast' with whom they were dealing. Not given to suspicious bent nor to scurrilous activity, these men were honestly intending to consummate a business deal irrespective of who originated the proposition. Failure was not a contender in the scheme of things, provided all participants equally shared the fall.

Late in February of that year, having weighed all the pros and cons, I approached Ted, when he was most vulnerable, early morning after a night of revelry. "Ted, when am I going to see some disc sheets from this deal that Gary is working", I said, knowing full well that the data was non-existent,. "I need to study them for a few days to ensure their pedigree is good and have records back to manufacture".

His demeanor was somewhat sour and his reply was slow in coming. "I'm afraid, I can't give you any news of the documentation, as it appears that Gary has dropped the ball and negotiations with the Airline have been put on hold".

"What a surprise", I said sarcastically, "You know Ted, if everybody concerned had done their due diligence, before plunging headlong into something that they had no knowledge of, the situation that exists now could have been averted, and as you know my colleague in England, did some investigation into the viability of the deal and came up with a big negative."

"I will be seeing Gary tonight" he said indignantly, "and to tell you the truth, I will have it out with him as to why we haven't seen any evidence of his so-called negotiations". What a turn about, he actually has doubts about his *friend's*

integrity, I thought, as I stared at him with utter dismay.

"I suppose he is going to reimburse everyone for their time and expenses, not to mention making good the credit card debits" I said, trying not to sound too angry, but feeling it. "How will you address the subject? and do you intend to let the status quo exist? still living on the good will of our company and sucking us dry."

By this time Ted had a flush of anger which, did absolutely nothing when aimed at me, his comments should have been aimed at his buddy, not now, but prior to the culmination of this debacle.

"Irvin Shoemaker will be here today and we will both tackle Gary together and thrash out the situation, he owes Irvin a good deal of money for the use of his aircraft and Irvin owes some notes on it and doesn't have the funds to cover them, and don't think that Gary is going to get away with it". He added with more than a little chagrin, which I supposed was the whole ugly scenario, but at least we could actually see the end of all this nonsense if Ted and Irvin followed through with their confrontation of Gary that night and hopefully regain some of the monies spent on this superfluous venture.

Irvin arrived mid afternoon and parked his aircraft at the Opa Locka Airport to save parking fees at the larger airports and Ted drove up to collect him and bring him back to the office where we chatted informally for an hour or so. I think the object of the exercise was to try and off-set the forthcoming confrontation by keeping the conversation light and friendly, trying to hide the inevitable in the recesses of their minds, as I am sure both men were expecting a veritable brick wall to climb, one that bricks and mortar could not hope to compete with.

Their arrangement with Gary was to meet at the Hampton Inn on 36th street, where Irvin would be staying, sometime in the evening, the exact time I did not know nor did I enquire as to the hour, my only definite knowledge was the venue.

Ted and Irvin decided to leave the office in the early evening and from my observation, they would have dinner and talk over their strategy, before going to the meeting place. I did not envy their task as I knew that Gary's demeanor would be as always, laconic, not volunteering any information other than that already known by the trio and showing a stoic resolve to any form of intimidation, which I am sure was the mind set of Ted and Irvin.

As I was not privy to any of their conversation, I waited to hear Ted's version the following morning.

"How did your meeting with Gary go yesterday", I asked Ted, as he entered my office at the unusual late hour of 10 a.m.

"I can't begin to explain how I feel about the situation and Gary was his inimitable self and at no time expanded on any question we put to him and his answers were at all times non-committal, which made Irvin and me angry, to say the least." Ted said with a rather resigned tone. "I am sorry to say that the conversation degenerated into a shouting match between Irvin and Gary and escalated from there.

After Irvin had presented bills for aircraft fuel, landing fees and handling of the aircraft, Gary smiled and leaned back in his chair and asked what Irvin was going to do about it." Ted took a breath and I could see he was reliving the moments of trauma from the previous evening. "I was afraid that things were getting out of hand and tried to intervene, but I could see Irvin was near to bursting point, so I tried again to mediate, hoping that we could reach an amicable settlement, but it was too late". Again Ted sighed and took another breather. "At this point Irvin pulled an automatic pistol from his jacket and pointed it directly at Gary, with the threat that he would kill him if he didn't pay his dues as promised".

At this point I recollected that Gary did not promise one thing, it was Ted who did the promising on Gary's behalf and I wondered whether as a point of law if any of this would stand up in court .

"I was afraid that Irvin would carry out his threat" Ted continued, "Gary just sat there as cool and collected as anyone could be, given the situation, and told Irvin to do what he had to do". Another pause to regain some composure, then he continued. "At this point I was in a state of stark amazement and couldn't find words to say as this situation was too poignant for me and I was really lost for words, which, as you know is unusual for me, to say the least". His emphatic declaration as to his inability to speak, was quite a revelation and I intended to use that self denial to its full benefit, if and when the need should arise in the future.

"What did Irvin do then?". I asked, wanting to know the full extent and ramifications of the saga, after all it did affect me indirectly, my job may well hang in the balance should the company's solvency become a receiver's situation. I could envisage myself sitting in front of the appointed official being deposed under frequently pointed questions, trying not to sound tenuous, as indeed my full knowledge of the foregoing happenings would be vague to say the least. I tried to put the idea out of my head and concentrate on Ted's dissertation.

"He just sat there for several minutes with the automatic pointed straight at Gary, not wavering, just frozen in one position, I suppose he was reasoning with himself as to the folly or otherwise, of such an egregious act he was about to commit, which was obviously calculated and premeditated" Ted had just become an instant psychologist, making presumptions that could possible fit the scenario, but in no way could he know Irvin's state of mind.

To think that Ted did not know the potential outcome of a fierce confrontation with Gary was to be naïve, but it would suit his situation as a witness should the worst-case scenario come to fruition.

"Go on Ted" I said, "that can't be the end of the story, what transpired after the gun episode".

"Irvin slowly lowered and un-cocked the automatic, before removing the magazine, which he put in his overnight bag and as he moved towards the door of his hotel room, he half turned to look at Gary and said "You're not worth a bullet, you are the lowest form of life, a parasite of the worst kind and I hope you rot in Hell for what you have done to me and my friends", It was a very sad moment for me as I watched Irvin walk out of the door", Ted sighed and sat down as if he had expended all his strength, he then closed his eyes and eventually said "I must find Irvin as I don't know where he went after he left his room, I do know that Gary drove off in the direction of Miami Beach". He went out of the office and I did not see him again until the following day.

Events had come to a head, Gary had been exposed for what he was and probably still is, everybody, including myself had been taken advantage of by this scurrilous person, exposing the vulnerability of those who would embrace all who extended a hand of friendship and bonhomie, 'live and let live' being the maxim by which decent people strive to achieve in their everyday lives,

It must be said that all willing participants accepted the risks that any speculative venture offered, but those risks were calculated on having an even playing field to begin with and to have an unforeseen handicap such as that which Gary Adams posed, was not in the initial equation. Honesty and decency were two words that did not exist in Gary's vocabulary and should one ponder the ingratitude and disingenuous nature of the beast, surely if there was divine providence in the scheme of things, he would ultimately answer to that higher authority.

Irvin Shoemaker eventually lost his aircraft to his creditors and apparently, after that episode lost his penchant for flying and concentrated his efforts on his gunsmith business, perhaps driven by the thoughts of what might have been and possibly hoping that others may use his wares to a more effective conclusion.

Wally Grant was out one hundred and fifty thousand dollars which naturally put him in financial difficulty for some time and certainly did not endear him to Ted Landry for the remainder of Ted's tenure, jn the company, when it came to business arrangements, however, as always he took the loss with dignity and carried on with his life, giving no outward signs of his emotions nor airing his folly for his gratuitous donation to Gary Adams.

Jim and Roland' co-owners of the 'B and B' engine overhaul shop, also took their losses without too much indignation, although my latter conversations with them portrayed some embarrassment on their part for their involvement with such a character as Gary Adams and the feeling that they felt sullied by such a person would remain with them for a long time to come.

Ted Landry drove the company into bankruptcy and finally departed for his Texas home where not too long after, his eating, drinking and smoking took its final toll.

I moved into another technical aviation position with a very prestigious company and tried to put the past behind me, however my thirst for fact finding and general regard for the profession with which my entire life had been orchestrated, I decided to try and follow up on the nefarious Gary Adams and if possible, forestall any deals which he may contrive with unsuspecting victims.

Episodes such as the one described, have a profound effect on those who have been fraudulently used and it certainly changes ones outlook on ones fellow citizens. Trust becomes a word that cannot be easily given and taken and in the foregoing context becomes an extinct meaning.

Little did I know how events may turn out and I have no satisfaction in relating future revelations and sequels to this story.

The Hereafter

My very next indirect encounter with the ubiquitous Gary Adams was some months later in 1989 when I had occasion to call my friend Steve in the UK, as I had not heard from him in a very long time, perhaps due to the indecent UK telephone rates, but I rather believed that he was busy with his work and had his mind occupied by the more important aspects of life.

How one ponders things in retrospect often associating the past with the current day events, this was how my thought train was veering when I spoke to Steve that September afternoon.

"Hello Steve" I said, trying to sound upbeat, "Have you forgotten your old mates, or have you been squandering your money on vacations and good times."

"A fat chance anybody has in this country to save enough for a vacation, let alone have a good time" he said, meaning every word of it.

"I know things are tight over there Steve but is it really that bad?, I know from what my daughter tells me that the bare necessities have risen in price and petrol is prohibitive for anything but getting to and from work."

"It really is my friend, you did well to go to the States after your employment in Jamaica, I wish I had youth on my side so that I could go back abroad and save some money for that rainy day."

I tried to lead the conversation in a totally different direction, as I could sense the maudlin tone that Steve had adopted and I did not want to exacerbate the situation and turn what was meant to be a reasonable conversation into a griping session.

"Well what have you been doing with yourself, since last I spoke to you?", I said, hoping for a very different response from the previous one.

"Perhaps you remember asking me some time ago if I knew a man named Gary Adams" he said, trying not give away his innermost feelings.

"Yes, I do remember telling you to be cautious, if fate brought you both together, why do you ask" I said, feeling a heavy lump come into the pit of my stomach.

"Well he contacted me a few months ago and said he was a colleague of yours and he knew that we had worked together some years past and he would like to meet me and have a beer or two". At this point I held my breath, reliving the events of the not-too-distant past and thinking that I had heard similar phrases from others with whom Gary had used my name as a reference, to gain an advantage, albeit, to ingratiate himself with people who could be of assistance to him.

"Steve, I warned you about him and I knew you were a man who could not be cajoled or badgered into doing something, illegal or underhanded, so I did not appraise you of his nefarious business dealings here in the States", inwardly upbraiding myself for not passing on the details of Gary's skullduggery to Steve and others who he might encounter. I did not think for one moment that this scenario would manifest itself in England with my friends and associates. A lapse on my part, for which I was deeply sorry. How reprehensible of this man to use people the way he did, it was obvious that he would stop at nothing to get his avaricious way, leaving a trail of disillusioned and dissolute people in his wake.

My conversation with Steve lasted an hour and a half, during which time a story unfolded which, although it entailed more dastardly deeds, did not in any way surprise nor phase me, because of the extent to which I was attuned to the vagaries of Gary Adams and accepted everything related to me by Steve as irrefutable, incontestable and true to form.

The Presentation

Gary approached Steve by calling him at home, a number which by the way I had not given him, so I assumed he managed to remember Steve's name and looked it up in the telephone directory, or used the services of directory enquiries, whichever the case, it was an easy read for Gary, as no doubt he had been in a similar situation previously and used his inherent wiles to facilitate an introduction.

As Steve resided in Worcestershire, it was a good two to three hour drive from London to Evesham, so it was evident to me that to further his intentions Gary drove the distance without hesitation. It was also evident to me through my conversation with Steve that my name was not mentioned too frequently, perhaps to keep Steve's mind away from me, in the hope that he would not call me and ask too many questions. As it happened, Gary, once again, used his innate ability to direct any conversation with Steve in the direction, he chose, leaving much unsaid in his seemingly plausible commentary.

The enormity of the proposal, which he laid out, was one, which General Electric or Wal-Mart might have considered given the financial assets which both companies possessed, but for an individual to contrive a plan based on other people funding the enterprise was nothing short of incredulous. Gary's ego was as large as the proposal he made to Steve.

Luton International Airport was situated approximately ninety miles from London and boasted a very healthy revenue from the airlines which operated from there, mostly charter flights to the more exotic European countries and quite a few to the United States and the Caribbean. It was an ideal location for access from both the north and south of England, situated on the main north/south M1 Motorway.

Airport facilities at that time, catered mostly for Passenger aircraft and the terminals were very 'state of the art' buildings, with an attractive façade, which made passengers feel light and cheery as they wended their way to the check-in podiums, for the initial ritual process of their vacations.

Any observer with the understanding of airport operations would plainly perceive the complete lack of cargo and freight facilities and any entrepreneur with the knowledge of the surrounding commercial requirements for shipping goods and heavy freight, could certainly make a case for building a complex. With that in mind and having done the due diligence and business viability study, running the numbers for the financial strategy, a reasonable acceptable business plan would be manifest, with which to present to the potential investors. Local government officials, the Airport Authority and any regulatory body such as the CAA (Civil Aviation Authority) and Department of Transport, would of necessity be heavily involved in the oversight of any such enterprise. To this end one would surmise that its inception would be strictly on the level.

Taking all of the foregoing prerequisites and correlating the results with the known and unknown factions, would require a very articulate person, especially if that person were to create the model by themselves without any extraneous assistance from design and architectural engineers, local government departments, such as water, sewerage and utilities and any bureaucratic department whose job bordered on anything remotely concerned with the project.

For one individual to concoct a reasonable facsimile of such a diverse and complicated project, would, in every respect be exceptional and possibly unrivaled in the annuls of aviation history. Nevertheless, it happened at Luton Airport, in an overt way which confounds all logic and rationale.

Steve met with Gary at a prearranged venue to discuss the potential project and was completely enamored with the way in which it was presented and detailed. Steve intimated to Gary that it must have taken a great deal of time to assemble such an intricate plan, but Gary apparently shrugged off the veiled compliment and conducted a very feasible verbal presentation, with a caveat that drawings and an official business plan would be forthcoming, should Steve give his blessing to the idea as presented.

Later in my conversations with Steve, I was amazed to learn that not only did he accept Gary's idea, he agreed to take an active part in the project and assist with the initial negotiations with the mainstream players. Obviously my advice made not one iota of difference to Steve as he blatantly accepted the status quo.

I would not have believed that Steve could be that bamboozled by Mr. Adams and the only explanation I could conceive of, was that Steve was so determined to get back into the aviation business, as he had been away from the industry for a few years, that he virtually accepted any project associated with aircraft, especially if it presented him with a challenge. Little did he know what kind of challenge would be forthcoming.

The local Mayor's office was duly notified in writing, by Steve, of the proposed enterprise and in turn the planning committee was appraised of the impending written draft proposal from Gary, which in fact arrived at the Luton Town Hall in a timely fashion.

Several committee stages, of necessity, would have to review the draft proposal and true to the bureaucratic processes of local government, a few weeks elapsed before any decision was made to proceed to the next level. Further to the general committee stages, which would be to arrange a presentation from the principal proposer, a special delegated committee would be convened for that express purpose .of hearing, reading, debating and resolving any issues of note, from the final draft proposal. A final decision whether to proceed with the whole complex project, was promised in a timely fashion, by the Chairman of the delegated committee.

During the hiatus of the deliberation by the local council, Gary apparently disappeared for a prolonged period but kept in touch with Steve, so as to keep abreast of any developments from the local authorities.

Eventually a date for the final presentation was set and Gary once again arrived in Luton for the expose, which in the main was developed and written by Steve, who, fair to say, had previously won prestigious accolades for similar proposals and copious drawings, with explicit explanations and numerous foot notes were compiled for the event.

The venue for the presentation was the Town Hall in the evening of a very pleasant autumn day, thus the turn out for such a meeting was very good, with a representation from all interested parties and a good cross section of the citizens of Luton Town, as this meeting was designated a Public Hearing, which gave even more exposure to the proposal than otherwise expected.

The meeting was called to order by the Chairperson at 7p.m. and all the attendant committee members were introduced to the assembly by name and finally Gary and Steve were introduced as the proponents of the presentation.

Not to be phased, by the public gathering, Gary, introduced himself again, to the assembled committee and general public, perhaps hoping to gain some credibility from that very act, in the hope that showing his outward façade would somehow endear his audience to his proposition. Human ego is a wonderful feeling if channeled in the appropriate direction and not used as a means to an end, especially if that end is to suborn, cajole and misrepresent the truth.

Meetings sometimes become protracted and people with diverse views on a particular subject tend to digress, intentionally or unintentionally and in many cases cause the main thrust of the meeting to get lost in the mélange of vociferous activity, however the rendition which Gary Adams gave that evening was direct and to the point, the subject matter being rather too specialized for the general public to comprehend in one 'fell swoop', consequently, interruptions were few and he concluded his presentation in the time allotted.

Several basic questions were asked of Gary and Steve and both fielded them with succinct answers, which for all intents and purposes satisfied the questioners. Drawings and detailed graphics remained on show, where they were laid out on large tables and several people stayed to look at the prints, especially the prospective building contractors, whose job it would be to construct the buildings and associated roads and taxiways, should they submit their tenders and have them accepted as the prime contractors.

I was not privy to any of the documentation which was shown at the meeting, Steve did however prepare most of the exhibits and knowing his capabilities, I am sure everything was as it should have been, laid out and presented so that the lay men could understand the rudiments of the plan.

The Mayor thanked the presenters and told them that the scheme as presented was interesting and should it become a reality, would certainly bode well for the local community, providing much needed jobs for the local populous and ultimately create a comprehensive airport where all transportation, both passenger and cargo, could operate efficiently and generate prolific business opportunities, which in turn, could further the financial solvency of the Town through taxes and local spending.

Obviously, Gary was more than satisfied with the outcome of the presentation and the next phase of his operation, of necessity, would have to wait until a final decision was forthcoming from the local authority. Again he disappeared for an indefinite period, but kept in touch with Steve on a regular basis, to ensure a timely return to Luton, if and when the decision to go ahead with the project went in his favor.

Timing is of the essence and were it not for the disingenuous proposal, from a genuine 'confidence trickster' the project was certainly a viable proposition, one, which at that time, would have generated all the ideals put forward in the presentation.

My thoughts were of a man who could conceive such a viable project, yet not want to follow it through to its logical conclusion. Why would anybody not want to be part of an enterprise, where wealth, fame and fortune were available?, not just for the concept, but for the overwhelming satisfaction of seeing something built from the ground floor, upwards, to the pinnacle of final completion, something tangible that a community could thrive upon and ultimately be thankful for the innovators who precipitated the reality of their thoughts and ideas and brought about change to an otherwise dormant society.

What was the thrill, the excitement, the compulsion, to cheat, steal and cause mayhem in a community which did not deserve such treatment, where hard working people lived in a seemingly austere social climate, with little expectancy of wealth or fortune, trusting that the guardians of their future were worthy of their appointed offices and able to make the right decisions for the good of the people.

Three weeks from the date of the presentation, the committee unanimously agreed to proceed with the Airport Cargo Complex and invited Gary and Steve to the Town Hall, where the Mayor formally accepted their proposition.

Having achieved the preliminary objective of their proposal, the second phase was to have Gary accepted as the Principal Coordinator, who would correlate all the information required to initiate the building projects and additionally marshal the necessary funds to accomplish the task, however the oversight would be by the appointed heads of departments within the local council bureaucracy, with special emphasis on the accounting department, which would judiciously control the collecting and distribution of the funds.

It was again a situation where the persuasive powers of Mr. Adams had a profound effect on the Town Council, giving him a carte blanch authority to conduct his own portfolio, thus his virtual autonomy allowed him to raise funds from private sources, which would ultimately be augmented incrementally with funds from the local coffers, when a suitable amount for starting the complex had accrued, which could take a protracted amount of elapsed time and a great deal of effort.

Steve was not aware of the details of how Gary managed to coerce the accounting department to allow him to act as the medium by which he could solicit monetary contributions to the project, suffice to say he achieved his goal, with obvious ease.

How could a viable business unit such as the Luton Town Council allow a virtually complete stranger such authority, without so much as a background and credit check, something which any potential employee, whether white or blue collar, would have to undergo, in the normal course of events. It must have been a collective thought process, comprised of the core players in the council, or conversely a combined aberration of their mental stability.

Perhaps the involvement of a stalwart member of their society in the form of Steve Cannon was a sobering influence on their decision, that was the most appealing reason to me, but my bias would be evident, due to my long standing friendship with him.

The Collection

Raising funds for any project requires much patience and perseverance and the persuasive powers of a wizard. Gary Adams, albeit acting as an independent contractor, went about his task, with the able assistance of Steve, and made great progress in a very short time. Actual figures of monies collected from private sources were never divulged to Steve and how and where the deposits of said monies were made was somewhat nebulous and Steve never did find the answers, much to his obvious chagrin and I doubt if he was ever recompensed for his services to the project, something which I think, to this day, is a source of acute embarrassment to him as a professional person. My one hope is that Steve did not lend Gary any financial backing, but that is something else that will never be known and I never would enquire of that subject, lest I lose a good friend.

Two or three weeks elapsed and Gary and Steve worked feverishly to build up a rapport with local business people and canvassed both ground and air freight companies, the larger ones of which were more than interested and the promise of future financial help, once the project 'got off the ground' was very encouraging.

At this time in the on-going charade, Steve Cannon had absolutely no idea of Gary's insincerity and fraudulent intent, consequently he worked very hard to bring the enterprise to fruition and once again he was in his element, back in the aviation scenario, conferencing, communicating and generally gathering as much influence as he could muster from potential willing participants. At no time did he directly handle the financial negotiations, as Gary insisted on keeping the financial dealings under one hat, his!.

How the incoming money was siphoned off,? where was it deposited,?where was the financial oversight from the local council,? who if anyone colluded with Gary,? are questions, the answers to which, will probably never be known.

In mid winter of 1999, Gary Adams took leave of the English countryside and vanished, as if from the face of the earth. I cannot imagine the total embarrassment of my friend Steve, who, 'left holding the baby,' to paraphrase a well known and well used saying, was absolutely overwhelmed by the unconscionable, reprehensible and crass way which Gary Adams had cheated and misused his loyalty and devotion to the project. I have no doubt that a man without a conscience, such as Gary Adams, felt not one iota of remorse.

Assuming that the funds absconded with, amounted to several hundred thousand English pounds, it is safe to again assume that the Town Council of Luton in the County of Bedfordshire, had many sleepless nights thereafter and much finger-pointing in the committees and formal assemblies was more than apparent to the unwitting bystander.

Steve went on with his life, hopefully a wiser man, with a memory of what had gone before, he had certainly gained a lesson in humility if nothing else, he did however, assure me that he would follow up with some discreet enquiries in the European theater and endeavor to find out if Mr. Gary Adams was working the continent, in the vain hope of forestalling more of his reprehensible deeds.

Steve and I kept in touch and mused over the whereabouts of Gary, but all the information which filtered through to us was from third party sources, which at any given time, was 'old news,' but several stories evolved which appeared to be bizarre to anyone other than the people he had embezzled, cheated, misused and those who had the misfortune to cross his path, socially and otherwise, the memories of which events would be indelibly scribed in their hearts and minds.

Rumours

In the ensuing months, my curiosity was piqued by various reports of Gary's activities, most of which emanated from people with whom I was in regular contact within the U.S., however, the reports were from tenuous sources and mostly involved his alleged activities in South America, Africa and latterly in Europe.

One report from a very reliable person in Texas, who was indirectly associated with the Miami affair, told of his purported dealings in Brazil, which if true, were par for the course with Gary Adams and epitomized the way in which he dealt with whomever he came into contact.

FATE

Introduction

Perhaps it was the fact that our squadron was the general duties, day and night all weather operational squadron, accepting all the mundane duties of Quick Readiness Alert (QRA) or any other duty which the prima Donna squadrons could not handle or anything which the Air Ministry deemed non priority but needed immediate attention, or perhaps it was the collective fundamental psyche of the personnel that made up this collection of dedicated airmen and airwomen, that eventually created the 'happening' or as the Air Ministry would call it a 'Contravention of Queens Regulations' which would camouflage a host of formal or informal anomalies, allowing the bureaucratic arbiters a high degree of latitude allowing them to apportion blame and recriminations for any untoward occurrence, whatever the situation, without reproach or redress from those to whom it was directed.

At this point it would be germane to say that the stage, which of necessity, must be set, to enable the story to be viewed with an enlightened vista and give the uninitiated, an insight into the environment which over many years of evolution has become the norm, which does not give rise to any intelligent or logical thought processes, as many rules and regulations borne of tradition, are fraught with illogical and unintelligent edicts, which in many cases become the precursors of laws and rules which govern the lives of the masses.

Tradition dictates the military mind and renders all other ideas and thought processes sterile and creates a mind- set uncharacteristic of acceptable logic and rational humane behavior, the Royal Air Force being no exception to the rule. However, as the Junior Service, it has had less time to foment the consequences of its actions and in part relied on the Navy and Army to lead it through the maze of bureaucratic jurisprudence and military regulations. To this day, it is forbidden by 'Queens Regulations' for an airman to leave his horse unattended and at all times must produce, on request, a clean and polished saber. At this point I rest my case for the reasoning behind any military actions and consequences thereof.

Chapter 1

Modern fighter aircraft take on the mantle of many varied roles and differ in sizes from the very small interceptors to the multi role heavy fighter aircraft. The aircraft in question, was of the latter class and of an ilk approaching obsolescence, but nevertheless an integral part of the mosaic which encompassed the air defense network around the British Isles, which hitherto was essential in the pattern of strategic international defense planning, which, being part of the NATO alliance, was of global significance to the member countries.

Gloster Javelin fighters were heavy, under powered, dirty, ugly relics of a bygone age of jet fighter aircraft, operated by two crew, a pilot and navigator, seated in tandem yet still classed as modern and in 1958 that was the case, in the sense that it carried modern weaponry in the form of two infra red seeking missiles, pod mounted, one on each wing, outboard of the landing gear doors and two 30mm Hispano guns mounted one in each wing, which for all purposes made it a formidable shooting platform, if and when it could reach a reasonable altitude from which to operate.

This aircraft required a protracted period of time, as jet age aircraft go, to reach an assigned altitude and the fact that it was underpowered, made the effort all that more burdensome, for the crews, because of its inherent sluggish, ungainly performance and mechanics, because once on terra firma it was a beast to maintain, rearm and prepare for flight. Generally it was a poor apology for what might have been.

What might have been, was a very high speed, twin engine delta, thin winged advanced fighter of classified performance, unequalled in its range and ordinance capabilities, one which could have outclassed any machine of its type in the military world and been a proud protagonist of a subsequent line of super fighting aircraft.

Original design specifications were of a futuristic machine, capable of roles hitherto unreachable by modern technical prowess and the pride with which the design team postulated its potential, was nothing less than awe inspiring and nationalistic exuberance was of monumental proportions.

The raw actuality of how the Gloster Javelin aircraft became the lame-duck war-horse of the Royal Air Force was laid squarely at the feet of the incumbent Minister of Supply, who managed to subvert the plans and aspirations of the designers and proposed manufacturers, to a level, which can only be described as degrading. Ostensibly the main reason given by the 'Government of the day' and as always, inaccurately reported, by the press and media, was that fiscal restraints proved to be the overriding factor for the non-production of the originally designed and proposed aircraft.

A British House of Commons, select sub-committee was then convened to asses the situation and to review the original proposal, ultimately to report its findings to Parliament and suggest intelligent, cogent alternatives bound by the monetary constraints of the Treasury, which although, never published, must have been a miserly amount to have rendered the original concept to one of abject inconsequence, lacking the quintessential merits of a modern fighting machine.

The Parliamentary decision, however ill conceived, was communicated to the selected Manufacturer, the normal procedures of formal bidding by an esoteric collection of Industrial Partisan enterprises, having been summarily dismissed, due to imposed time constraints by the sub-committee, which composed of a number of middle-aged academics, the majority of whom were totally incompetent to render a decision concerning the security of the nation, which is what this resolution amounted to, in the light of the role for which the proposed aircraft was intended.

Once a Manufacturer had been selected by a Government Department, it would be commercial folly for any enterprise, to ask to be excused from the project, on any fiscal or production grounds, however expedient. Situations of this genre, were fraught with inconsistencies and political overtones, not the least of which was black listing.

The dichotomy, which the Board of Directors, of necessity, faced, in the dawning of the accolade, which had been so incontrovertibly, placed squarely on the incumbent company, was in all respects, daunting.

On one hand, the technical and administrative preparation required to orchestrate such an undertaking was daunting and the budget constraints, imposed by the bureaucracy, created manifold problems which had to be addressed and resolved in a very short space of time. Considering the fact that the issues revolved around national security, the subject would require a concentrated effort from the management team to put the concept into a production mode. Should everything happen in a controlled methodical manner and the prototype meet all the requirements and the pre production and ultimately the final product meets all specifications, this would not in any way shape or form guarantee a perfect flying machine which would meet the preconceived ideas of the stoic establishment. All was not a mood of confidence.

On the other hand to place the company in a position of denial and exclude itself from the contractual commitment placed upon it, would undoubtedly create a situation where many politically biased, partisan companies, would withdraw their industrial cooperation and many of the products required to continue day to day production of aircraft and related components. This apparent set back, coupled with the fact that subsequent Government contracts would not be forthcoming, did nothing to reduce the consternation,which confronted the Board of Directors.

A fait accompli, in all respects, compliance with the will of the bureaucratic establishment became the rule. The hapless manufacturer, put its best effort into the fraught project, surmounting the obstacles, as they were manifest and the prototype production of the proposed final product occurred one year after its conception. The all weather, day and night fighter, became the Javelin, the original formal designation of which was Javelin F(AW). Mk1.

Chapter 2

When any production aircraft enters military service it was customary to complete a series of trials encompassing all facets of service from hot and cold weather, to combat, ordinance and maintenance exercises, creating a program of a highly comprehensive nature, during which period, the anomalies could be found and remedial action taken in a timely fashion.

It was fortuitous that a team of experienced airmen was selected to carry out the prescribed trials, which took place between 1954 and 1956, when it officially entered RAF squadron service, which included basic flying maneuvers and culminating in full combat readiness exercises, which would allow the aircraft full service certification, ready for active service with a squadron, composed for the specific purpose for which the aircraft was intended.

Squadron leader John Waterman, was given the task of leading the trials team and his experience at the Experimental Aeronautical Establishment was unsurpassed by his peers and his appointment was another creditable accolade to his fine career as a Royal Air Force pilot and officer.

At this juncture, it must be pointed out that the Javelin aircraft was the precursor for all future delta wing aircraft, in that it was the pioneer for the all-flying tail, which in essence meant that the pitch attitude, was controlled by the elevators situated on the horizontal stabilizer which was atop of the vertical stabilizer and coined the phrase 'T tail'. This configuration was hitherto untried and hence unproven and due to the unique construction of the flying surfaces, the most rigorous testing would, of necessity, be protracted and tedious.

John Waterman, a veteran test pilot, took the lead role in the initial flight testing and after two consecutive flights, during which the emphasis was on the performance of the basic handling of the aircraft, in which all flying controls were tested for fundamental response and sense, he became aware of a restriction in the movement of the horizontal stabilizer at certain cruise speeds and at times had to apply significant pressure on the control column to counter the abnormality and the electrical trim mechanism on the stabilizer, which was designed to counter the air loads on the flying surface, did not produce the desired effect.

Reporting the undesirable flying capabilities of the aircraft to the manufacturer's design team, John Waterman became a target of some adverse criticism, from the representatives of the Ministry of Supply, who pontificated on the delays which such criticism would cause to the eventual production of an acceptable production fighter. Unwarranted as it was, the feelings of the bureaucracy filtered through to the Ministry, who in turn disseminated the somewhat distorted information to the Air Ministry, the contents of which were relayed to the Air Force Chiefs, responsible for the Testing program and ultimately to Waterman himself.

It is the way of all information media, to create a chain of truths and partial suggestions, so that, as with legends, all pertinent facts become so distorted from its inception to contemporary recounting, so that in the final analysis what was indeed an initial factual report of observations made by John Waterman in the pursuit of his profession, became an illogical, disingenuous, malicious, denigration of his findings, which did nothing to assist the test program in any respect.

To be scrupulously fair to the Design Team, they did all within their limited power and resources to mitigate the apparent flying control problems and made several adjustments to the mechanical linkages and reset the electrical trim mechanism of the horizontal stabilizer and all ground functional tests proved satisfactory and the aircraft was prepared for a routine test flight to re-check the system in question.

In the interim Squadron Leader Waterman, much to his consternation, was summoned to Command Headquarters to give an account of the problems, which he had encountered during the test flight and to answer those derogatory remarks made by those faceless bureaucrats sitting in their mahogany floored offices, impervious to all the real world events and smug in their unwitting insincerity.

The visitation to Command Headquarters went without any untoward recriminations and once an explanation had been given, all in attendance, which included the senior resident staff member, one, Group Captain Roger Pearson, a man of impeccable flying reputation and a man with more than a modicum of common sense, were satisfied, an amicable conclusion was reached and the hearing adjourned.

Waterman reflected on the day's events and dismissed it for what it was, a group of self-appointed adjudicators, imposing their self-importance on a subject that they could not even remotely understand. it was comforting, however, that his superiors were behind him all the way, their comprehension of the absolute facts being infinitely more intelligent, than the conclusions reached by their Ministry counterparts, which said nothing for the Government of the day.

The following day saw another flight to ascertain the viability of the designers adjustments, and although there seemed to be some improvement in the handling characteristics of the aircraft, it did not feel right, yet John Waterman continued with the air test. Reaching a time when he was about to conclude the flight regime he applied aileron and rudder to initiate a turn to fly a reciprocal heading, which would take him back to the airfield. As the control pressures were applied, the control column jammed and although the turn maneuver was initiated, an opposite control input could not be given to bring the aircraft back to level flight, however much force, the pilot applied to the control column. This situation was fraught with potential danger, as the theory and practice of flight dictated, that unless an equal and opposite control deflection occurred, the aircraft would continue turning and roll into an attitude which in an unknown, unproven aircraft, could be disastrous.

Waterman's reaction was instantaneous, reducing power, on both engines to alleviate the gravity forces on the airframe and flying controls, he exerted as much force as he could on the control column and realized that the way his weight was distributed, the leverage obtained would not be adequate to overcome the mechanical lock on the controls. Although he was six feet tall and weighed close to two hundred pounds, none of which was excess fat, he transferred both feet to the left rudder pedal and heaved with two hands on the control column. This feat of dexterity in such a confined space served to neutralize the turning effect of the fighter and with a sustained effort eventually brought the aircraft to a wings-level attitude. As the aircraft again plowed its path toward the home base airfield, the tension of the preceding few minutes of physical endeavor was felt in every fiber of his body and the mental effort, with which to regain his physical control, seemed to drain him emotionally.

John Waterman was no stranger to flying anomalies, but in this instance his thoughts immediately reflected his concern for his personal safety and that of the aircraft. He quickly dismissed the thought and with a totally professional demeanor, he adjusted his physical position in the seat to the normal flying posture and trimmed the aircraft mechanically, checked all his flight and engine instrumentation, which appeared to be functioning correctly, then, he deployed the air brakes and slowed the aircraft to a speed where he could comfortably lower the gear. As his main concern was for airframe distortion, he had to mitigate further potential damage and it was correct procedure to reduce stresses on all flying surfaces and continue to home base in that mode. Once the gear had been extended and all indicator lights were normal, he keyed the microphone and called the airfield traffic control to request fire and crash tenders and a straight-in approach to the active runway, to preclude having to make any procedural turns, before landing.

The touch down and roll out was without incident and the aircraft was brought to a stop at the end of the runway where all emergency vehicles moved to their relative positions around the fighter. There was no evidence of fire and steps were quickly positioned, enabling the pilot to open the canopy and exit the aircraft.

Chapter 3

Wing Commander Peter Rich was in attendance at the aircraft steps. It was his duty as Operations Officer of the day, to be where the problems occurred, a duty which was normally quiet and much of the time could be spent in his comfortable office in the control tower, on stand-by for any untoward event which may present itself during the course of a normal day's flying program.

He took Waterman by the arm and led him to his waiting land rover and drove him back to his office to debrief him on the recent incident. This was standard procedure and would culminate in a written report made by the pilot, prior to any future flights of the aircraft, which would allow time for a complete inspection of the fighter, to ascertain the apparent problem and carry out any remedial work required.

Having completed his report Waterman, proceeded to his living quarters which were off the airfield, in the officers quarters adjacent to the Officers Club, which was almost one mile from the aircraft park. He did not feel much like recounting the story to his wife, as the more he thought about the train of events, the more he felt ill disposed to people in power who would risk life and limb to attain a completed project at any cost. His wife was a stalwart in times of adversity, however, he did not want to spoil the rest of the day and evening, by dwelling on this thought provoking subject, although, tomorrow would be another confrontational day and one to which he was not looking forward.

Group Captain Roger Pearson and Wing Commander Peter Rich were waiting for Squadron Leader Waterman at Station Headquarters (SHQ) both were in a somber mood and once in the CO's office, Waterman was ushered to a chair adjacent to Pearson's desk, it was apparent that the situation was urgent and needed immediate attention and questions were fired at him in quick succession. At one point, after half an hour, it was patently obvious that Roger Pearson's questions had been prompted by a higher authority and the direction in which the questions pointed could only be interpreted one way, which did not auger well for any subsequent dialogue between the two, as innuendo and veiled threats did not sit easy with John Waterman.

Peter Rich was feeling very uncomfortable, as he was in attendance to act solely as an observer, or witness, whichever the context may be, in the light of the seemingly, over zealous, line of questioning and to give very little input, as his role, was quite passive and occurred after the event, however, he thought that it was unreasonable to try and apportion the blame for events on John Waterman, as this was a man who gave his all to his profession and put his 'life on the line' daily, so that others could fly safely.

In essence, the whole thrust of the questioning alluded to the probability of incompetence, by John Waterman and brought his qualities as an experienced airman, into question and impugn his integrity as an honorable RAF officer.

The remainder of the interrogation was curt and eventually became ineffective as Waterman's innermost being had been irrevocably offended, thus his answers became guarded and clinical, hence the continuance of such a farce was of little consequence and the meeting was adjourned. To the credit of the senior officer he apologized for the tack which he had taken, during the inquisition, suggesting that the questions were not of his agenda and his brief was from a more senior source, which was obvious from the outset, but nevertheless abhorrent to men of honor and integrity.

As John Waterman strolled back to his office he mulled over the events of the preceding hour and resolved to keep his faith and not succumb to the unwarranted attacks on his professional abilities, his one regret was that he was not carrying someone in the navigators seat, to witness the events, which in retrospect he could not do at the preliminary stages of the trials, in any event his word was his bond and good enough for those contemptible people, who confined themselves inside the walls of their cozy offices, never to taste the core of reality, never to hold the reigns of life, always to remain in the shadows of the unacceptable bureaucratic deity.

Having completed his report of the preceding day, Waterman called his flight test team into his office, where he informed the assembly of the all prior events, including the mornings visit to SHQ, leaving out his personal thoughts, it was however, obvious, to the assembly that fingers had been pointed, albeit without credibility and all inwardly sympathized with their leader.

Proceeding with the future flight test program was essential and he directed the maintenance engineers to liaise with the design team and reconcile the problems at the earliest possible time, as speed was essential to further the production schedule and regain the already forward momentum of the now thwarted itinerary.

Modifications were effected on the flying tail mechanism, which was eventually modified, in later years, from electric to electro-hydraulic actuating mechanism, the extensive ground checks proving satisfactory, the aircraft was prepared for a further flight which John Waterman insisted on flying, as he would not allow his number two test pilot to risk something, of which he had prior knowledge and could understand from his previous encounter, an edge which could mean the difference between life and death.

Chapter 4

The following day was a clear bright day as autumn days could be in the south of England and the test team busied around the Javelin making the final pre flight preparations, all awaiting the arrival of the pilot with marked anticipation.

At noon John Waterman approached the aircraft and ably assisted by the attendant mechanics, he climbed the steps to the cockpit and settled into the ejection seat and strapped in securely. This done, he went through the flight test check list, which normally took a minimum of thirty minutes, every little item scrutinized and cross checked, nothing missed in an effort to create a clean platform from which to launch the next flight and preclude any single problem, however minor, detracting from the main thrust of the exercise, which was to check the flying capabilities of the aircraft under all conditions of weather, flight control configuration and any other requirement laid down in the flight test schedule.

Opening the throttles on the take off run John Waterman, concentrated on the correct procedural check list to retract the gear and clean up the flying controls, which would enable him to reach an assigned altitude in the optimum time, giving him the most time possible to conclude the proposed test regime. Attaining the desired height, he started the test check list and quickly went through the opening sequences and proceeded to the next set of tasks, which required high speed cruise configurations, so as with other potential high-noise situations, he set a course which would take him directly over the coast and thence out to sea, where he could continue his schedule without fear of reprisals from the local populous around the vicinity of the airfield.

Performing as well as he could expect, Waterman concluded the test schedule in a time that was more than satisfactory and he felt as if a positive achievement had been accomplished and called the airfield on the assigned VHF frequency to clear his approach back to the airfield.

At a certain point in time, after his concentration had lapsed somewhat following the intense period of the test profile, John Waterman had a gut reaction, which told him that all was not well. He checked all flight and engine instruments, to ascertain if his feeling had a basis for concern. All appeared normal and he set a course for home and tuned his radios to the correct communications and navigation frequencies in readiness for his approach to the airfield.

Having set up all the required inbound procedures, Waterman detected a faint burning smell, which had penetrated his oxygen mask, which he had worn during the test portion of his afternoon's flying. Quickly releasing the catch holding the mask to his face, he inhaled lightly to try and define the origin of smell. Without an aircraft red or amber warning light to identify the overheat, or fire warning location, he had no idea from where the acrid smell emanated. Donning his smoke mask he continued to try and identify this apparent anomaly, to no avail. He quickly keyed the communications switch on the control column and informed the air traffic control tower at the base, that he suspected that he had a fire in the aircraft, but could not isolate the area of concern. This done, he turned his attention once again to the warning light panel, no light was illuminated, so he hypothesized as to what might cause a potential fire and not enable a red or amber warning light and could not come up with a logical explanation.

Except for the area in the main avionics and hydraulics bay, all other areas had, overheat and fire warning devices and a fuel leak would be more easily detected by the fuel gauges and associated warning systems, which would give prior notice of low contents, low pressure and any abnormal feed to the engines. Theorizing that the problem was in the equipment bay, he voiced his thoughts to the control tower at the airfield and although it was normal procedure to have emergency and crash vehicles standing by, he reiterated the situation and requested all emergencies services to be in attendance when he landed.

Twenty miles short of the runway, Waterman could see tiny wisps of smoke entering the cockpit from below his ejection seat. Reporting the situation to the control tower, he was directed by the senior controller, on the advice of the senior duty Operations Officer, to assess the situation and if he deemed the aircraft was in danger of being a fire hazard, prior to, or on landing, he should fly back over the sea and ditch the aircraft after ejecting from a safe height. This was standard procedure when an unknown element, such as this apparent fire, could preclude a safe landing or possible endanger the local villages, which were in the path of the approach to the airfield.

Decisions of the kind that had to be made on a value judgment and of necessity, quickly, are rarely the right ones in retrospect, however, his experience told him that to, abandon the aircraft at this juncture, would not in any way, enhance the safety of the any subsequent aircraft manufactured for the role it had been given, without the prior knowledge of the potential hazards, so his conclusion was to bring the aircraft back to the airfield and present the anomaly, to the designers and their puppeteers, so that remedial action could be taken to prevent future occurrences of this magnitude.

Hoping for a straight-in approach and landing, to be as normal as it could be under these adverse conditions, his one thought that the fire would not spread to other areas of the aircraft, in the next few minutes, made all his landing preparations that much more precise and purposeful. Conveying his decision to the control tower, he proceeded to carry out his final cockpit checks for landing.

As Waterman eased the aircraft on to the glide slope and adjusted his speed and descent rate, by use of the air brake spoilers, he trimmed the flight controls and throttles and proceeded to the lower the flaps and the landing gear. All appeared to be working correctly, however, the acrid smell of burning was penetrating his smoke mask, making him very uneasy, as his thoughts turned to the potential threat of his oxygen supply becoming an instant fuel for the fire, should the heat rise to a degree where spontaneous combustion would occur, nothing else would matter if that happened, so he concentrated on his final approach and landing, which must, of necessity, be as smooth as possible and the roll out must take him to a position where the emergency vehicles could reach him, in a minimum possible time. He thanked his maker that he did not have a ventral fuel tank fitted underneath the aircraft, as he would have had to jettison it prior to landing, which would have facilitated finding an open area in which to drop it and that would have consumed more precious time, something he did not have.

Final radio calls with the control tower completed, with emphatic assurances that all emergency equipment was in place, Waterman aligned the fighter with the active runway, which had been designated for his straight-in approach. Fortunately, the weather was good with a negligible cross wind and visibility perfect. Reducing engine power to a level where the aircraft would subside on to the runway without too much lateral movement, the aircraft settled on to the tarmac runway without any tire squeals or any significant rubber burn, in fact it was a text book landing.

As soon as the aircraft weight had settled on the gears, Waterman operated the ground spoilers and applied the brakes, hoping that the brake units would not overheat and cause additional potential fire hazards. Coming to a stop less than half way down the runway, John Waterman quickly disconnected his flying suit from the oxygen and communications systems and releasing the locking mechanism, grabbed the handles on the canopy, at the same time looking around desperately for the fire tenders and emergency crash vehicles. Glancing to his rear he saw smoke billowing up from the under belly of the aircraft, at the same time heaving on the canopy to allow a rapid exodus from the cockpit. To his abject amazement, it would not move and all the effort applied from his more than ample physique, would not budge the canopy.

During the time in which the aircraft had come to a stop the fire tenders and crash equipment were en route to the scene, however the time taken for the vehicles to reach the burning fighter was inordinately long and as the pilot struggled to release the canopy, it was patently obvious that the situation was becoming fraught with many dangers, not the least of which was the imminent explosion of the aircraft as the fire propagated through the airframe and would eventually reach the fuel tanks.

Time seemed to go so slowly as Waterman struggled to open the canopy and as his strength was waning he glimpsed a figure running up the left wing to his cockpit position and within seconds of the fireman reaching the canopy, it was released externally and he was assisted out of the cockpit and down the rear of the fuselage and over the trailing edge of the wing and once again on terra firma, he ran to a safety position where Peter Rich was waiting with his utility vehicle.

When John Waterman had gained some of his usual composure, he turned to Rich with a quizzical, inquiring look, which required no words and begged the question as to whether or not he was meant to survive the ordeal. Peter Rich could not meet the gaze of Waterman and quickly looked away in an effort to hide his own indignation for the actions of those responsible for the present situation and his own complicity, however reluctant, his part had been.

Waterman was incensed with the whole situation. He could have died, others could die, if remedial measures were not taken to ensure that modifications were embodied to obviate the anomalies, which he had encountered, during extensive flight testing. His resolve was to make a full detailed report to his superiors and follow up with a further, more pointed document to the Air Ministry and Ministry of Supply.

Investigation into the primary cause of the aircraft fire, concluded that the residue from the starter cartridges, which were composed of raw cordite, ignited and spread through the main equipment bay where hydraulic oil added fuel to the fire and created a potential disaster.

At this juncture, it should be stated that when the Javelin, all weather, day and night fighter, finally went into squadron service, in 1956, the same starting system was still maintained, as in the early prototype series of the aircraft and numerous fires were reported and in some cases the entire equipment bay was gutted and extensive repairs of necessity, were undertaken, which were time consuming and expensive.

Later series (Marks) of the Gloster Javelin, were modified with a more modern type of engine starter system, which proved to be just as lethal as the original system and to mitigate the problems arising therefrom, a small panel was cut into the main equipment bay panel, underneath the fuselage which had to remain open, until both engines were started, then checked by the ground mechanic for signs of fire, before being secured, prior to aircraft dispatch. Furthermore no fire warning and extinguishing system was ever fitted to the aircraft, in the areas of concern.

Chapter 5

John Waterman spent many days preparing his presentation to the Air Ministry, which out of courtesy, was first passed to the Station Commander, Group Captain Roger Pearson, for his observations and to his credit, he passed it on to the relevant department at the Air Ministry, unabridged.

The outcome of the report to the Air Ministry was the suspension of John Waterman from the flight test program, whilst remaining in the administrative post, supervising the day to day activities of the program and the disposition of personnel. This situation did not sit well with him and he accepted the status quo under sufferance, but not before he had made the Station Commander fully aware of his feelings, to which Roger Pearson empathized, but was unable to countermand the Ministry edict, much to his displeasure.

Up to this particular point in time, Waterman had been the primary test pilot of the program, which now became a redundant feature and needed to be addressed immediately, so he called his deputy, Flight Lieutenant Andrew Pine, to his office, where he quietly and directly laid out the situation, at the same time confiding his displeasure at not being able to assist in any subsequent flying, so it would behoove the incumbent, Andrew Pine, to accept the situation unconditionally and apart from the flying, Waterman would support him without reservation.

A flying program was drawn up and a strict schedule plotted for the next few weeks, which would hopefully allow them to catch up with the proposed Air Ministry schedule, if all went according to plan.

Two days later, the prototype aircraft was again declared ready for service and a flight test schedule was prepared and was thoroughly scrutinized by both John Waterman and Andrew Pine and the pre flight briefing covered all the flying profile eventualities and safety precautions, which were to be strictly observed.

The pre flight cockpit checks were completed without any glitches and a start up time was given by flight operations, which would allow Andrew Pine to have a final few minutes to go over some salient points of the flight test with John Waterman. Engine start clearance was given by the Control Tower, five minutes after midday and apart from a light wind of five to ten knots from the north, the weather was fine for flying. As the aircraft taxied out to the end of the active runway, John Waterman looked on with some foreboding, hoping that all would go well with this seemingly, ill-fated aircraft. Walking slowly back to the operations office, he could hear the two jets winding up for the take off run and less than a minute later it was airborne and heading for the assigned test area more than one hundred miles to the east of the airfield.

Exactly forty three minutes into the flight test program, air traffic control, received a call from Andrew Pine, reporting some abnormal flight characteristics being experienced during several test maneuvers, which were more pronounced when executing turns. He requested that John Waterman be brought into the communication loop, to advise him on any actions which he might possibly take, to mitigate the anomalies. Five minutes later Waterman was in the control tower talking to Pine, trying to pinpoint the apparent reasons for the problems currently being encountered over the coastal area. Finally it was mutually decided to bring the fighter back to base, with a view to discussing the incident, at a debriefing, with designers and engineers, subsequent to the aircraft landing.

Completing the radio calls, Waterman turned to leave the control tower, intending to return to his office and assemble the relevant personnel, for the upcoming technical discussion on matters relating to the most recent revelations on the fighter's performance. He was about to open the exit door, when he heard a high-pitched voice from the tower speaker, repeatedly calling, 'Mayday'. This distress call was from Andrew Pine who, for whatever reason, was experiencing difficulties and was in dire trouble. Racing back to the controller's position, he grabbed the hand microphone and immediately requested Pine to detail the exact problem. Replying in a quavering, yet controlled, voice, Andrew Pine, told Waterman that the controls appeared to be locked and he could not trim the aircraft to a straight and level attitude and he was losing altitude rapidly. With a reasonable altitude above his terrain, it was possible to recover the aircraft, given certain conditions of flight control configurations, but time was of the essence and discussing alternate ways of taking remedial actions apart from those already taken, was superfluous. Making a snap decision on the known facts, Waterman ordered Pine to eject from the aircraft, if control of the aircraft could not be immediately regained.

Awaiting the expected affirmative reply, which was not transmitted, hence not received. Waterman, again repeated his ejection order. No reply, just the static noise that was the norm from the speaker, when no voice transmissions, were in progress. Another more emphatic transmission from Waterman was not acknowledged and he suspected the worst, trying to qualify the reasons for no received messages from Andrew Pine. He immediately instructed the attendant controllers to alert all emergency vehicles on the airfield and advise the Search and Rescue helicopters to stand by for immediate dispatch. Silence, permeated the control room as everyone finished their emergency calls and all strained their ears, hoping to hear a transmission from the stricken aircraft. After ten painful minutes the worst fears were realized, as an emergency telephone call was received by the chief controller, from the county Police Headquarters, informing the station that an aircraft had crashed in an open field, forty miles east of the airfield and rescue vehicles had been dispatched to the scene. As their were no immediate eye witnesses to the accident, nobody could say whether or not the pilot had ejected safely and this was the crucial issue at the present moment.

With a racing heart beat, John Waterman, sat in the control tower listening to every radio call to and from the control tower, the rescue helicopters were already airborne, and were in constant communication with all the ground emergency services and it would be a few more minutes before anything would be known of the fate of the Andrew Pine.

Six minutes later a transmission was received from the first rescue helicopter, reporting that as they were approaching the sight of the crash, smoke and flames could be seen billowing from the ground and fire tenders from the local town were on the scene and were actively involved in an attempt to extinguish the fire.

A further transmission, ten minutes later, from the rescue helicopter, confirmed the fact that the pilot had perished in the crash and subsequent inferno, with no chance of rescue. An awful death for a young dedicated airman, who, although mindful of the risks taken by a test pilot, died needlessly, to fulfill a political and economic expedient.

John Waterman felt empty, could he have averted this tragic accident?, did he do enough to convey his fears to the hierarchy ?, would anyone listen to his pleas for further investigation into what must be an inferior aircraft ?. Self deprecation filled his thoughts as he pondered the imponderable. No machine is worth a life under any circumstances. If only he had done this or that!, if only he had made more of the previous problems !. How can an honest man come to terms with an anathema that was manifest in the 'Halls of Power', a sightless, soundless canker, spreading its pernicious tentacles to the far corners of the nation's heart, without redress or accountability, pontificating its credo, like some omnipotent deity. Perhaps there was a day of reckoning for those who would perpetrate such misery and pain. Let it be soon!.

Waterman left the control tower, a very sad, discon-solate man, not knowing how to atone for the death of his comrade, nor how to approach the future, with a positive agenda. His input to the remainder of the flight test program, would be superfluous and with that thought uppermost in his mind, he resolved to resign his commission and try to make the general populous aware of the shortcomings of those who held the reigns of power.

Squadron Leader John Waterman resigned from the Royal Air Force and wrote a very poignant, factual, no holds barred, book, centered around his experiences as a test pilot on the javelin project, a book that was received with much consternation, in the ranks of the faceless bureaucracy, however, official critique of the journal, intimated that the book was written by a resentful man, who had no regard or patronage for his country. A sad testament for a man whose dedication in the ranks of test flying, was universally known and applauded.

Chapter 6

The Javelin, All Weather, Day and Night Fighter entered squadron service with the RAF in the late fifties and was plagued with many problems from the outset, not the least of which, were fires in the main equipment bay, complete generator power failures, flying control defects, hydraulic failures and many more anomalies of a lesser nature. To try and enhance the poor engine performance a twelve and a half percent reheat was added to the engines and could be used only at high altitudes, otherwise increased fuel consumption and actual loss of power was experienced. Many aircraft crashed, some with loss of life, others the crews safely ejected and became members of the Martin Baker club, Martin Baker being the manufacturers of the ejection seats.

It was the accepted practice to have crews from foreign countries flying with the RAF and the 'Exchange Program' as it was termed, provided for a pilot and navigator crew from the United States Air Force to fly with the Javelin squadron as a team and once the basic training on the aircraft had been accomplished, both airmen joined a squadron in East Anglia, a very rural part of England, yet suitably appointed for a fighter base.

Captain Paul Johnson, a pilot and Captain Richard Carey, a navigator, were the airmen assigned to the squadron and both were very happy at the proposed tour of duty with the RAF, which could extend to three years.

Their families were transported with them from the States and both were given very spacious living quarters, much to their satisfaction. All boded well for their stay in the United Kingdom.

During the first two years of service with the squadron, both airmen seemed to adapt themselves well to rigors of the English weather and the vastly different lifestyle of the Royal Air Force. They had survived some rather serious incidents during this period together, but managed to remain alive, whilst at least two squadron aircraft had crashed, with the loss of both airman in one aircraft. At that particular time, the ejection seats fitted to the fighters were of a type where a certain altitude and airspeed were required, to successfully eject from the aircraft. It is prudent to say that a ground level ejection seat for the aircraft, was in the planning and development stages at the time of this crash and would be expeditiously, put into service, as a result of a subsequent crash.

The final year for the two American airmen was quite uneventful and as the end of their sojourn in the United Kingdom approached, they prepared to return to their own country of domicile, in fact, with furlough time accrued, Richard Carey decided to return to the USA one month prior to his actual tour of duty termination date and Paul Johnson would remain active for the upcoming month and the take his accrued furlough, with his family, in the United Kingdom, before returning to his native country.

Although Paul Johnson and Richard Carey were a pilot and navigator team, they did often fly with other RAF crew members, as duties dictated, so it was no untoward situation when Johnson was paired with different crew members for the remaining month, in fact he enjoyed the nationalistic banter between himself and the British crews, with whom he shared a wonderful rapport.

Stationed at the RAF airfield, were three squadrons, two, day fighter, Hawker Hunter squadrons and the Javelin squadron. One of the day fighter squadrons was the Air Force Aerobatics Squadron, named, the Black Eagles, as all of the aircraft were painted a gloss black with the squadron crest emblazoned on the vertical fin, which made a very impressive livery. Treble three squadron, as it was officially designated, was the pride and joy of the RAF and performed many aerobatics displays at home and abroad and became famous for its high degree of precision formation flying and did much for the recruitment image of the RAF.

Watching the practice performances of treble three squadron day after day, over the airfield, the other two squadrons became cynical and somewhat envious of the prima donna activities of the 'Pride of the Air Force' not the least of which were the members of the Javelin squadron, who had the mundane tasks of training flights and many night flying activities which culminated in a week's stand by duty (QRA.) every month, including week ends, none of which treble three were encumbered, hence the animus reactions of the onlookers.

It was with a euphoric sense of relief and expectation that Paul Johnson prepared to fly his last sortie with the RAF, a practice interception with another aircraft from the squadron, which would take off five minutes prior to his take off and then, with the able assistance of his navigator, he would carry out a precision radar interception and lock-on his infra red acquisition missiles, after which, the aircraft would return to base and that would be the culmination of three years exchange service with the Royal Air Force.

Brian Browning, a Flight Lieutenant navigator, would be accompanying Johnson, on this auspicious flight, a very accomplished, experienced navigator, one who in the distant past, had safely ejected from a stricken aircraft at a height of fifteen thousand feet, and both he and the pilot had lived to tell the tale.

As both pilot and navigator prepared to accept the aircraft, by signing the official aircraft log, in the 'Line' office, they were approached by several enthusiastic squadron mechanics, who, with light hearted banter, proposed that Paul Johnson should give the squadron a boost and show the number one aerobatics squadron, just how to perform precision aerial maneuvers. With a non-committal smile and nod he walked with Browning to the aircraft and mounted the steps to the cockpit, at the same time as his navigator climbed the back steps and walked up the fuselage to his position behind the pilot.

Start up, taxi and take off, was uneventful and the javelin proceeded to climb to its assigned altitude, from which the practice interception would be initiated. All went well with the planned operation and the fighter headed for base. At this point, Paul Johnson asked Brian Browning if he was willing to give the squadron personnel a show of aerobatics over the airfield. Browning concurred, with the provision that it was kept simple and that they did not exceed airframe limits. Without detailing his proposed maneuver, he continued his approach to the airfield.

Approaching the airfield, Paul Johnson called the control tower and asked permission to execute an aerobatics maneuver over the airfield, explaining to the controller that this was his final flight with the Royal Air Force and he would like to give the squadron members something by which to remember his tour of duty with the squadron.

There was an air of anticipation, as the line mechanics waited outside the line office, for the imminent return of the fighter. The hangar staff, were also standing around the neatly organized miniature gardens, which made the normal drab grass landscaping, more pleasing to the eye.

The low pitch drone of the two engines, throttles open, announced the arrival of the aircraft over the airfield. At two hundred feet, level with the center-line of the runway, the fighter approached the mid point, adjacent to the line office and hangar, at an approximate speed of three hundred and fifty knots. Pulling the control column back into his midriff, Paul Johnson lifted the nose into a climb, initiating an intended loop. As the fighter attained the vertical attitude the speed was rapidly falling off, but the flight controls still commanded an inverted attitude to complete the loop. Reaching the apex of the loop, the aircraft stalled and under no circumstances would the aircraft go into an inverted posture. Falling from the sky with no perceptible forward airspeed, to give a required, positive lift component, the aircraft took on the motion of a dead leaf falling from a deciduous tree. Gasps and muffled cries from the onlookers, only accentuated the dramatic situation being enacted, in what seemed to be, slow motion.

At approximately two hundred and fifty feet from the ground the cockpit canopy was ejected, quickly followed by Brian Browning, the navigator, in his ejection seat. A split second later the pilot ejected and his ejection seat could be seen traveling at an angled trajectory from the aircraft. Hitting the ground with an earth trembling thump, the Javelin exploded, producing a red and orange fire-ball which billowed into the clear blue sky. In the intervening period, the two ejection seats were plummeting to earth, one parachute deployed, indicating that the particular seat had operated correctly, allowing its occupant to separate from the seat and parachute to earth and the other seat could be seen with only the drogue chute streaming, a precursor to a failed ejection.

Brian Browning hit the ground, a few seconds after his seat, but at least thirty feet apart, he was injured, yet he quickly divested himself of the parachute by hitting the quick release mechanism on his harness. Although dazed, he looked around for some indication of the pilot's position and focusing on an object fifty feet from where he stood, he could make out the human shape of Paul Johnson, sitting motionless in the ejection seat. He ran, as best he could, to the pilots seat, arriving out of breath and heart beating at an abnormal rate. In the background he could hear the sirens of the crash vehicles approaching his position.

Brian Browning did not dare release the harness which held Paul Johnson in the ejection seat, for fear of causing more trauma to the obviously severely injured pilot, he just stood by the seat, praying that there was life remaining in the man, which a few moments before had been the pilot of the flying machine which now was spread over a wide area of the airfield, the main fuselage burning in the crater, created by its impact into the soft grass area, several yards north of the runway. The emergency medical vehicle arrived at the site of the somber scene and quickly moved to the where Paul Johnson sat limp in the ejection seat. Having made a quick check of the vital signs, the Medical Officer pronounced the pilot dead, and gently shrouded Paul Johnson with the white drogue parachute.

There was much commiseration and spoken feelings of sadness, from all fellow officers and squadron personnel, at the Air force Station, for a man who was well thought of, yet the feeling of futility outweighed all else, as the death of Paul Johnson was totally avoidable, should not have happened, could not be justified, emphasized the unacceptable capabilities of a purpose built fighting machine and more poignant and ultimately more important, removed a devoted father from a wife and five children.

The outcome of the tragic event, precipitated the immediate installation of the more advanced 'Ground Level Ejection Seats' and by Air Ministry edict, precluded the use of the javelin for any aerobatics maneuvers other than those required to fulfill the normal function of its approved role.

In the 'Circles of Power' and in the corridors of those who would postulate on matters of which they had little knowledge, it was mooted that this modern, high technology, purpose built, over financed, under powered, utility fighter was never intended to perform aerial combat calisthenics, especially those for which it was ultimately, fatefully used. History would prove the justification for the critics of the Javelin fighter, without any notable subsequent accountability by those who would remain in the shadows of bureaucracy.

FLIGHT INTO OBLIVION

The night was clear and bright, but there was a sharp chill in the air as the four whispering Rolls Royce Tyne turbo prop engines accelerated to move the heavy transport aircraft from its jetway at Brussels International Airport en route to London Heathrow Airport (LHR) with one hundred and fifty passengers (souls) on board, all with different thoughts and aspirations of the arrival in London for whatever purposes.

Captain Joe Rayner turned to his first officer and called out the first of his taxi check list as the aircraft made it's lumbering way out onto the main taxiway, where the nose wheel steering system would, with dexterous application from the pilot, guide them to the end of the active runway, in readiness for full power take-off and flight to England.

As the aircraft moved along the taxiway, the third crew member, the Flight Engineer, busied himself with the tedious tasks of checking fuel systems, oil and pneumatic pressures, air conditioning and pressurization settings, in readiness for the upcoming journey.

The engines tone changed, as the throttles were advanced to the take-off position, through the beta ranges, the blades coarsening off to bite the cool night air and pull the aircraft into the night skies with a minimum of effort and optimum thrust ratings.

Although the flight to England was less than two hours duration, the weather forecast for the en route portion of the flight was good, however, the terminal area around London was marginal and some degree of fog was forecast for the late evening and as it was late January, the weather could change in a very short time and dense fog was the aviators enemy in all senses of the word.

Lifting off the runway the Vickers Vanguard aircraft climbed out of the airport with a very positive rate of climb, heading for its assigned cruise altitude of twenty thousand feet, where it would level off and the course and heading adjusted, tracking its way north west to the English coast line and thence on into the London area.

Flight Attendants made preparations for the serving of liquid refreshments and an evening snack, which in any event was a hurried affair, due to the short duration of the flight and speed of delivery was all important to both served and servers alike.

Having reached cruise altitude, the throttle settings were adjusted and the second phase of the flight sector was initiated. Radio communications with London Control Center were clear and concise and the terminal weather was reported as still marginal.

With all the other European flights in and outbound from London, there appeared to be no undue cause for concern to the flight crew and all settled down to the normal routine of en route flying, making radio calls and adjusting flight controls and autopilot settings and generally keeping a visual watch on the surrounding skies for intruders into their airspace, which rarely occurred, due to the rigorous and accurate controlling in the various communication centers.

As the miles went by, the weather at LHR deteriorated to an almost diversionary situation, which would reroute the aircraft to an alternate airport where the weather would be acceptable for a visual landing. It was at this time that the captain would, of necessity, make the decision to divert or carry on to the original destination, hoping to make a landing in a clear weather slot, as fog has a tendency to clear momentarily and is patchy in nature and an experience airman would weigh the odds, erring on the side of safety, knowing the risks which might occur, should the wrong decision be made at the wrong time.

Easing the throttles back to begin the descent into the London area, the captain called the weather service center for an update of the foggy conditions at LHR. Terminal conditions were variable but leaning toward the worse rather than the better, a decision had to be made at that point whether to proceed or divert to an alternate airport.

To ask any human being to weigh a given situation and resolve it in a timely fashion, when a potential disaster was a possible outcome of making the wrong one, is by definition, fraught with consequential errors.

Bringing to bear all of his professional experience of many years flying the line, Captain Joe Rayner, had, what was considered to be a workaday problem to solve, many of which he had been confronted on many occasions and had taken in his stride, the majority of which were correct decisions attesting to his formidable airmanship. If some decisions were incorrect they were of an isolated nature and in no way would have been catastrophic, as remedial measures were taken to immediately correct any disparity.

Any event, which could impair 'safety of flight' was dealt with in the most expedient way, erring always on the side of safety.

This was one of those times when the apparent consequences of proceeding to LHR could be corrected, if at the final approach phase the weather became too bad to make a precision visual landing, a 'go-around' could be initiated and in concert with Air Traffic Control, diversionary procedures would be immediately instituted.

As the approach to the airport continued, a decision by the captain to land, of necessity, had to be made, given that all the variables were known, not the least of which was the deteriorating weather at the airport.

All landing checks completed and the appropriate passenger cabin signs illuminated for the final approach, Joe Rayner had initiated the landing sequence, again, having been advised by ATC that the weather was closing in and many incoming international flights were seeking alternate airports.

Apparently, not to be dissuaded by the London Airport curse, Captain Rayner continued the landing phase, without recourse to the First Officer nor the Flight Engineer, both of whom reportedly, never queried the Captain's decision to proceed in the worsening weather conditions.

At a point where the aircraft attitude becomes critical, just prior to touching down, the normal course of events would be that the pilot in command, whose responsibility it is to land the aircraft, look for external visual references, as well as monitoring the flight instrumentation, together with the First Officer, to ensure correct flight control landing configuration, while the Flight Engineer would manipulate the throttle settings to ensure correct engine thrust on landing.

The radio altimeters were reading ninety feet, the barometric altimeters were indicating one hundred feet, but the discrepancy was not of such a magnitude as to create undue concern at that point. It was however, a crucial factor in the subsequent events, on that murky, dismal, foggy January evening.

Not being able to see the runway clearly, the decision to go-around was made by the captain and all four throttles were pushed fully forward. All four motors accelerated to full power and the aircraft responded to the alteration in pitch attitude from the pilots control column, the nose of the aircraft moving up into the climb mode.

Air Traffic Control provided the flight path information which the aircraft must follow in order to make another attempt at a landing, at the same time the controller advised the captain that the weather was again deteriorating to a category three visibility, which did not allow for the propjet to land as it was only certified to a category two coupled approach only.

As the aircraft ascended to a height conducive to ATC requirements, the flight crew were finally discussing the situation in a rather emotional way, both the first officer and flight engineer opting for the diversionary situation, which at that moment in time, would take them to the alternate London Airport of Gatwick, which in elapsed time would take less than fifteen minutes. The captain however, was of the opinion that a second attempt at landing at LHR, could be made before electing to divert to Gatwick airport.

Unable to be persuaded otherwise, the captain continued the flight pattern, which would put the aircraft in an approach mode for landing. With the landing gear already down and locked and all flight controls in the landing configuration, the throttles were retarded and a shallow pitch down attitude was initiated.

Thick fog at this time covered the whole airport and ATC advised Captain Rayner to divert to the most convenient alternate airport and to advise them when en route. What possessed the captain to ignore the advice, cannot be explained and he instructed the first officer to read the final approach checks, which, although routine, had to be repeated for every landing, irrespective of the number of approaches made on any given flight.

Calling ATC for final approach, he was advised that the surface wind speed was negligible and runway visibility was down to twenty meters and vertical visibility down to fifteen meters, which was not conducive to attempt a landing. Ignoring the ATC advisory, the aircraft continued its perilous descent.

The First Officer was monitoring the barometric altimeter, resetting the Q.F.E to double check the airfield altitude, frequently tapping the instrument panel adjacent to the instrument, to ensure no sticking errors in the mechanical working of the altimeter.

The Flight Engineer was diligently observing the engine instrumentation and throttle settings, particularly the EGT (Exhaust Gas Temperature) engine oil temperatures and hydraulic pressure gages to ensure all were in acceptable parameters.

At a predetermined height the First Officer called out the barometric height in feet and the Captain monitored the radio altimeters, the readings of both theoretically should coincide, however, there was still a discrepancy between the two and as the aircraft was still approximately two hundred feet above the runway, a further go-around could be initiated.

It is a possibility that both the barometric and radio altimeters could have calibration errors, which cumulatively could create an unacceptable discrepancy and would have certainly created a warning situation on the flight deck, precipitating diversionary operations and hence avoiding any potential hazard.

It can only be surmised that Captain Rayner perceived that the radio altimeters were more accurate of the two indications available, thus he continued the original flight path to the flare height (approximately 60 feet) where the throttles would be fully retarded to allow the aircraft a smooth transition to the runway.

It was at this point that the aircraft dropped at an obtuse angle and hit the concrete with a thundering, grating, metal tearing roar. The engines exploded as the propellers dug into the impervious runway, immediately causing the engine fuel lines to rupture, spewing fuel into the night air, which spontaneously ignited to create an eerie scene, as the light from the flaming fuel reflected off the now dense swirling fog bank, creating gross monsters which changed form with the ever moving fog.

As the aircraft came to rest, the entire fuselage was burning with such intensity, that parts of the now fractured hull appeared to be dripping molten metal, which in reality was debris from the openings in the torn fuselage, burning as it fell to the ground.

The aircraft had a broken back and in the light of the inferno, several passenger corpses could be seen, motionless and burning. This macabre scene would remain forever, in the memory of those who witnessed the scene that fateful night.

All emergency services were alerted prior to the crash, however, due to the reduced visibility, the distance the emergency vehicles were from the crash site and the raging fires once on site, precluded a timely rescue attempt.

All passengers, flight and cabin crew perished in the accident and questions as to the cause of the accident, which was laid squarely at the feet of the flight deck crew, reasoning that ultimately, the ill judgment to make an attempt to land in such diminished visibility, was the sole contributor to the horrific catastrophe.

It was reported from various sources. none of which were confirmed, that the radio altimeters were reading thirty feet high at the critical decision height and the barometric altimeters were marginally high, but within acceptable tolerances.

The demeanor of the aircraft Captain and the thought processes which precipitated his decision to land that night, when his vast experience would have told him otherwise, could only be conjecture as the human element, with all the attendant foibles, in any precarious situation, cannot be discounted and remains a paradox to which there is no answer.

TURN OF EVENTS

Except for the monotonous whirring of the ground power units, the morning was relatively calm at this first line fighter station in the heart of the East Anglian countryside. Blue skies and a crisp nippy temperature boded well for the forthcoming day's flying, which would be somewhat of a record breaking performance if everything went well and everyone was on their mettle.

Out on the hard standing the twenty two sleek, black, fighter jets sat majestically awaiting the time when the pilots would climb into their cockpits and begin the exercise which was becoming a daily ritual,. but all were of one accord when such a prestigious display was about to be presented to the world, patience and resilience were the order of the day.

Squadron Leader Richard Gaunt looked anxious as he waited for the flight crews to settle down in the flight briefing room, which was situated in the annex to the large hangar, at the south end of the airfield. Three minutes to briefing time and he felt a tightening of the stomach muscles, which, although was a usual event, the feeling seemed more intense, which he attributed to the upcoming finale which was about to be enacted over the airfield in full view of those who would judge the number one aerobatics team as to its merits.

The other tenant squadrons of the airbase would be watching intently this morning as the Black Eagles of the Royal Air Force premier aerobatics squadron would endeavor to carry out a maneuver that hitherto had not been attempted by any aerobatics team worldwide and because of the degree of difficulty and the emotional drain on the flight crews, would probably never again be performed.

During the protracted briefing of the squadron, Richard Gaunt was trying to put on a brave facade, although his innermost thoughts were that the law of averages would eventually catch up with their challenge of men and machines, defying the laws of gravity and physical capabilities of man-made flying phenomena, high speed precision procedures were at best difficult, at worst impossible, however the one consolation was that the past few weeks of practice had gone reasonably well, but the most difficult of all aerial calisthenics was about to be performed in the blue skies over the English countryside.

The briefing concluded, the pilots prepared to disperse to their respective aircraft for a rehearsal, which would be unique in the annals of aerobatics. Previous rehearsals had been rigorous and prolonged, sometimes twice a day, sometimes preceded by classroom instruction, which hopefully would indelibly instill in their minds the procedures which culminated in a precision flying routine which would last for forty minutes. Today that routine would conclude with the piece de resistance, the arrow-head loop formation with twenty two aircraft, never before seen anywhere in the world.

Richard Gaunt was a meticulous person, an excellent pilot and a fist rate officer and his hand-picked, team were equally adept at airmanship and every man a proficient

Air Force Officer and their respect for the Squadron Commander was manifest in their daily actions both on the ground and in the air. This morning everyone involved with the operation would be on their mettle and Squadron Leader Richard Gaunt was in the vanguard of the formation, leading from the front, setting an example to all who followed.

Half an hour to go before engine start up. Richard Gaunt shouted a final word of encouragement to the assembled crews, then grabbed his flying helmet, affectionately known as a "bone dome", and strode through the hangar doors followed by the other twenty one airmen.

The walk to the aircraft dispersal area took only a few minutes, during which time each crew member would be mulling over in his mind the upcoming practice with all the attendant possibilities which might and could occur, as they created their aerial pageant, which would be seen by all those spectators willing to watch the flying circus about to be enacted above the airfield at precarious heights, with very little margin for error.

The Squadron Commander climbed the steps of his aircraft, which were perched on the left hand side of the cockpit and leaned over to the far side to steady himself, preparing to lower himself into the ejection seat. This done he continued to settle into a comfortable position, if comfortable is an operative word in the vocabulary of a jet pilot, as any fighter ejection seat is at best, uncomfortable, at worst, debilitating. As he moved his legs into a position where his feet would fit into the rudder pedals with ease, he found that the leg restraining straps were twisted around the lap straps and to unwind the tangle, he did some one handed finger exercises which were normally successful, if done in a very strict sequence, he considered this dexterity to be equal to that of an accomplished pianist. Having arranged the safety straps he proceeded to strap himself into the seat with the aid of a mechanic who was perched precariously over the canopy ready to hand him the shoulder harness when required, which was sequentially after securing the lap straps.

Next, he checked the quick release mechanism for correct operation and finished the settling in process, by putting on his helmet and connecting the communications jack and oxygen tube. Finally the pig skin gloves were pulled on and pressed into the recesses of each finger web until total comfort was established, which was so important, when a good tactile feeling for controls and switches was imperative and sometimes critical in the overall cockpit procedures. Professionalism was a code word with Gaunt and his demeanor was always reflected in his actions.

Once settled, a glance around the cockpit, checking the general appearance of the instruments and controls, reflected his familiarity with his environment and anything out of place would register immediately and could be addressed before carrying out his formal cockpit checks. Everything OK, now to the instrument settings and control checks, which would take another fifteen minutes, give or take a minute, this was dependent upon whether or not he encountered any technical squawks (defects) in the process. Flight controls checks for elevator, aileron and rudder completed, he selected the tower frequency on his radio panel and called for a radio check, which was five by five (OK). All was ready for the squadron to begin its activity, which would last for a period of forty five minutes from chock to chock (start to finish).

Selecting his squadron communications frequency, with which he would control all the aircraft, he checked with all individual pilots to establish their flight readiness status after which he contacted the control tower to request permission to start engines and obtain a final wind and weather check, which was all part of the official pre flight protocol. Gaunt knew that all was well and it remained to be seen if these enthusiastic airmen could match the perfection of the day which Mother Nature had bestowed upon the gathered assembly.

Gaunt gave the order to start engines at exactly 9am and the hiss of the IPN starters could be heard for miles, followed by the whine of the compressors and turbines as the engines ran up to self sustaining speed. As the engines stabilized the noise settled down to a low roar as the crews allowed the engines to drop back to idle temperatures and all cockpit instruments to come to operational readiness. Outside, the clouds of hot gasses and smoke from the initial ignition of the kerosene in the combustion chambers of the engines, was drifting over the green expanses of the aerodrome and would disappear over the boundary fences to annoy the local population of the nearby village.

The ground crews busied around the aircraft, closing observation panels, removing ground power trolleys from the aircraft and notifying the pilots, by hand signals, of the state of aircraft after which they stood by the aircraft awaiting the signal to remove the wheel chocks in preparation for taxiing to the assigned area where they would form up in a pre take-off pattern.

Having given the signal to remove chocks, Gaunt spoke to the squadron over the radio and gave the order to taxi and take up position at the operational readiness area at the end of the active runway. All aircraft engines increased power as the fighters taxied in single file to the holding position.Gaunt taxied his aircraft on to the runway centre line, moving a few hundred feet down the runway to allow the other aircraft to form up in triangular formation behind him, ready for the mass take off, which in itself requires precision and dedicated concentration.

Each pilot aware of the extreme dangers of what was about to commence, would be subconsciously enacting the safety procedures which would be instantaneously put into action should any untoward situation arise during the flying performance. Safety first was always the motto of the conscientious airman especially of those who grew to a dignified old age.

Awaiting the order to take off heightened the tension of all concerned and pumped the adrenaline through the veins of the incumbents bringing them to a total awareness of their environment, which inevitably honed their perception to an inordinate degree bringing with it a sense of well-being and a modest confidence in their ability to complete their assigned roles.

At the command from Gaunt to advance throttles to take off power the noise outside the cockpit was deafening but the pilots heard only the muffled roar of the jets through their insulated helmets and could easily distinguish verbal commands from the leader without difficulty. Within seconds of the first command, the order to release brakes and roll was given and twenty two, first line fighters of the Black Eagle squadron took to the air in an arrow head formation with perfect equilibrium and grace.

Climbing to 10,000 feet, the squadron maintained the formation and leveling off at that altitude they settled down to consolidate their arrow head formation and tighten up any items of deviation and spacing which may have been caused by the climb.

For several minutes Gaunt led the flight straight and level to a position twenty miles from the airfield, where a final briefing on the upcoming maneuvers would be given to the crews.

There is a point where the tensions of the preparations, once executed, melt away in the concentration of the assigned tasks and Richard Gaunt felt the burden of command recede to a point where he could perform like a well oiled machine, knowing that all the contingent parts would function in unison with his will. This was the ultimate in flying, only the birds of the air could rival it.

Level at ten thousand feet, the sky was clear and the sun was reflecting through the cockpit canopy, making the pilots pull down their helmet sun visors, which would eradicate the unwanted rays and allow more precise visual contact with the remainder of the team, especially the adjacent aircraft.

All was ready and the order was given to turn in formation, which facilitated all aircraft banking to the right together maintaining the arrowhead configuration and flight level of ten thousand feet. The reciprocal course would take them directly over the airfield, where at a given command the pièce de résistance would be performed.

All eyes fixed on the aircraft ahead and fleeting glances to both left and right, helped to maintain the separation necessary to keep the squadron in a stable situation in readiness for the coming maneuver, which would be at a height of fifteen hundred feet, where everything would be clearly visible from the view point of those spectators watching from the sanctuary of terra firma.

Precisely at noon the Black Eagle aerobatics squadron appeared over the airfield at the appointed altitude and as the mid point of the runway was reached the lead aircraft nosed upwards, starting the ascent, auguring the most ambitious aerial stunt ever attempted in the history of international aerobatics.

To loop five or even nine aircraft in formation, maintaining the precision of professional performers, is, in itself, a feat of excellent airmanship, however to loop twenty two aircraft with the same precision is nothing short of magical artistry.

From the ground the aircraft appeared to be carving a symmetrical pattern in the clear blue sky and only the noise of twenty two jet engines, at climb power, disturbed the, would be, serenity of the scene.

All pilots were intently concentrating on their airspeed and distance separation from the adjacent aircraft and their relative position in the arrowhead formation. To fly in the inner confines of the formation was infinitely more demanding than flying on the periphery, where only the inside aircraft need be closely monitored, hence the more experienced aviators were chosen for the more difficult positions.

As the formation achieved the vertical portion of the loop, all was going according to plan and the arrowhead seemed to be a rigid entity, belying the fact that twenty two powerful, throbbing machines, were straining, as one, to achieve the ultimate, perfect objective.

Entering the top of the loop the formation appeared to be in a perfect position, confirmed by the radio silence of the leader, who only transmitted in those precarious positions, when absolutely necessary.

As the fourth row of the formation reached the apex of the loop the outer right hand aircraft of that line seemed to stall with an instantaneous piercing engine scream, which was heard by all spectators on the ground, immediately followed by the tail of the aircraft contacting the nose of the following aircraft which was situated at the most extreme right of the formation. Radio silence was interrupted with a muffled cry of alarm from the pilot in the stalled aircraft who proceeded to break from the formation in what was supposed to be a prearranged diversion tactic, should anything untoward happen during the performance. Banking steeply to the right, trying to avoid the following aircraft, the pilot of the stalled aircraft overcorrected, creating a more serious attitude problem, precipitating loss of lift and thrust simultaneously, which could not be corrected in the fraction of a second given for those situations and in the blink of an eye the aircraft impacted the ground with a deafening explosion as the fuel ignited spontaneously.

At the moment of alarm from the stricken aircraft, the leader, assessing the situation with lighting speed, called for the formation to break and fly the prearranged danger alert diversion and considering the attitude of his aircraft at that instant, inverted and ninety degrees from the vertical, his reading of the situation was remarkable. A split second later he banked and pitched the fighter to his assigned compass position area where he would issue the order to the squadron to reform and fly the prescribed pattern for sequential landing, thus allowing all aircraft to touch down and taxi to the dispersal in a controlled orderly fashion.

At the moment of crisis, all airmen had to respond to the emergency, as if it were second nature and the rigid discipline with which they were inured resulted in a complete recovery and landing of the remaining twenty one aircraft. To say that the individual emotions of the pilots were calm and relaxed would belie the fact that, having seen a comrade and friend die a traumatic death, they were inwardly glad to be alive and did not balk from the thought.

Fire tenders and ambulances attended the crash site which was situatedfive hundred yards from the hangars in an area that was open grassland and fortunately did not obstruct the main runway. There was nothing to salvage, as the crash made a deep crater in the ground and debris was scattered over a wide area around the crater and nothing remained of the pilot that could be readily identified. The area was quickly cordoned off and the attendant medical unit drove to the dispersal to attend the living, after all, that was their forte and one that was carried out with unerring selflessness and pride.

Richard Gaunt dropped from the bottom rung of the aircraft ladder and removed his helmet and gloves, handing them to a mechanic, who had marshaled his aircraft to the correct parking spot. This done, he strode quickly over to the aircraft, which had accidentally been an unwilling and unwitting party to the frightful incident. Still in the cockpit the pilot, one, Flying Officer Julian

Green, sat ashen faced and perfectly still not wanting to be moved from his dire thoughts. Gaunt quickly ascended the fighter's ladder and proceeded to remove the shoulder and lap harness from the incumbent and unplugged the oxygen and communications jack plug, so that Green could emerge from the cockpit unobstructed.

Gaunt said very little to the daunted pilot as he urged him to get out of the aircraft, which he did with very lethargic movements. Once on the ground the Squadron Leader took the Flying Officer by the arm and force marched him over to a two-seater training fighter, which had been brought to immediate readiness on the request of Gaunt, which he ordered by radio as he taxied in to his parking position.

The Medical Officer was waiting at the steps of the aircraft, where he made a determination that Julian Green was physically fit to continue flying, first having made a cursory examination of the subject.

Gaunt assisted his charge into the cockpit and quickly moved around to the opposite side of the fighter trainer where he propelled himself into the adjacent seat and assisted by a ground mechanic deftly strapped himself into the ejection seat. Checking that his co-pilot had been ably assisted into his harness he waved the mechanics away and called for engine start up. The ejection seats in the trainer aircraft were side by side, which meant that Gaunt had to stretch across Green to actuate certain switches in the starting procedure, as his flying partner was reluctant, if unable, to follow check lists and pre flight protocol, as his demeanor, appeared somewhat unreadable and pre-occupied.

With engines running, the brakes were released and the aircraft taxied to the active runway where without much ado, take off power was achieved and the fighter trainer took to the air with an all too familiar roar.

Richard Gaunt had many things on his mind as he ascended into the heavens, however the most urgent matter was to get Julian Green back to the world of reality as soon as possible, as the trauma of the recent events had taken its toll on the young man's psyche and as with all psychological disturbances, the sooner one comes to terms with them the quicker the healing process. The act of enforcing this remedy was an age old tradition and one which was found to be an acceptable, albeit a harsh, therapy and better for the young airman to realize the fact now, than to dwell on the aftermath of the tragic events, in which he was an unwilling participant, the repercussions of which could end his flying days forever.

Once into a normal cruise altitude, Gaunt handed over control to his charge, watching intently as the man became more aware of his environment and reacted in a manner, which pleased his chaperone. Normal training procedures ensued and after half an hour all seemed well with Flying Officer Green and satisfied that nothing more could be achieved at this time, Gaunt instructed his co-pilot to return to the airfield, where other very pressing matters awaited them.

Back in his office. Richard Gaunt again took on the mantle of Squadron Commander and proceeded to arrange the coming events into matters of priority. Julian Green was put in the charge of the Squadron Adjutant, one, Flight Lieutenant Roland Johns, who was given strict orders to keep the young Flying Officer under constant surveillance and report any untoward events which could give rise for concern for the well being of Julian Green.

Task one accomplished, he then telephoned the Station Commander, Group Captain Robert Horsfield, who had been waiting impatiently for a verbal report on the fatal accident. He instructed Gaunt to appear in his office at Station headquarters as soon as possible, where he and several other officers, including the Station Safety Officer, would receive the details of the foregoing accident.

Entering the Station Commanders office, Squadron Leader Richard Gaunt, suitably attired in battle dress uniform and peak cap, saluted the Group Captain then removed his cap and sat in a chair which had been positioned for him, in front and to the right of Robert Horsfield's desk.

After the Group Captain had inquired after the well being of Flying Officer Green, Richard Gaunt recounted the events of the morning leading up to the accident. All in attendance were quiet and very attentive and at no time did anyone, including the Group Captain, interrupt the dialogue. At the conclusion of Gaunt's report, the Station Commander invited an input from the assembled officers none of whom offered any questions or comments, except for the Safety Officer who said that he would visit with Squadron Leader Gaunt after the written report had been completed and prior to the formal inquiry being conducted.

As with all military events, written reports, would of necessity, be compiled and copied in triplicate, before being submitted to the Station Commander, who in turn makes out his own report and processes all copies through

Fighter Command Channels, which would ultimately end up at the appropriate office in the Air Ministry.

Dismissing all except Richard Gaunt, Robert Horsfield addressed the immediate question of informing the deceased officers family, which Gaunt would do personally, then proceeding to all the investigative work, which would have to be seen to be done, the findings of which would never be conclusive, as the remains of aircraft and pilot were beyond recognition.

All members of the aerobatics team would be questioned, the results of which would be recorded and filed. Technical bulletins would be issued for all aircraft to be thoroughly checked for any malfunction, before the next flight of the aircraft, in most cases, nothing would be found, nevertheless all must appear to be carried out which can be carried out, as the loss of a life should not preclude any avenue of investigation.

A topic of discussion which would inevitably be broached was whether or not the proposed and promised, twenty one aircraft loop would now take place at the forthcoming International air show, present at which would be the Royal Family, the Prime Minister and many other notable dignitaries. Group Captain Horsfield was of the opinion that more thought should be given to this maneuver before a decision was made to continue or otherwise and was adamant that should a decision be made to continue with it, any subsequent incident would curtail the maneuver immediately and would not be performed under any circumstances. This mutual agreement by Richard Gaunt and the Station Commander, ended the discussion and donning his cap, Gaunt smartly saluted his superior and leaving the office at SHQ returned to his own in the hangar adjacent to the airfield.

Having accepted the most unpleasant of all assignments, he picked up the telephone and called the home of the dead pilot, Flying Officer Jeremy Gould, however, there was no answer, so the ordeal of telling the parents would be delayed for a further few hours.

Jeremy Gould was a twenty five year old bachelor, who, having had a very good Private School education, had joined the Royal Air Force at the age of eighteen and excelled in his studies and flying abilities at the Staff College, after which he was posted to a first line fighter unit where he again made his mark as an Airman.

Selection for the RAF aerobatic team was very formal and required many referrals and testimonials from previous operational squadrons and establishments, but Flying Officer Gould made the team without much ado and his pride was unbounded when he learned of his acceptance with the premier aerobatics team, and his parents were overjoyed at the prospect of seeing their son perform at the show piece of the decade. Now all was but fond memories and the dreams of what might have been.

Chapter 2

The morning of the second day seemed to drag on and Gauntfound himself organizing the transportation of the dead pilot to his home town where his parents requested that he should be laid to rest in the family plot, in the local cemetery. Naturally he would attend the funeral, representing himself on a personal level and the Royal Air Force, formally.

Today there would be no flying as a mark of respect for a comrade and many pilots would catch up with their administrative duties, which tend to get neglected in the fervor of the day to day flying operations, albeit their enthusiasm for any kind of work, had been dampened by the events of the previous day.

After lunch and much report writing, Gaunt called the whole squadron together in the hangar and pilots, mechanics and administrative staff assembled to hear the Squadron Commander brief them on the fatal accident and to reassure them that the aerobatics practices would continue in the near future, in readiness for the day when the team would perform for dignitaries and public alike, at what was already being known as 'The Air Show of the Decade'. Much media coverage had been given to the upcoming event and television and news crews had been invited for a pre- show interview with the Station Commander and Richard Gaunt which was scheduled for the week prior to the show.

All squadron personnel were relieved at the news of the continuing practices and all knew how the death of a crew member, effected their endeavors to give that little bit extra in the hope that the end result would be a flawless exhibition of airmanship.

The weekend was coming up quickly and several items needed to be attended to before the usual stand-down on Friday evening and apart from essential duty crews, the squadron personnel would report back to work Monday morning next, for an intensive week of flying and preparation, which would be followed by a weekend dress rehearsal that would require all essential pilots, mechanics and administrators to be available and on duty.

It was the norm that the incumbent aerobatics squadron of the Royal Air Force were exempt from the usual fighter squadron duties, which the other squadrons were not too happy about, as it made extra work and more weekends on camp for all who had to participate, however in the event of an emergency, aerobatics would be shelved and the squadron would quickly come to combat readiness, hence all personnel were trained to move from the passive to the active environment without any undue inconvenience to the squadron routine, this was a testament to the thorough training regime to which all trades and general duties personnel were subjected, during the course of their military career.

It would be another week or two before the Board Of Inquiry convened to ascertain the cause of the death of Flying Officer Jeremy Gould and in the interim period all official reports would be assembled and held in abeyance for the Board to review and ultimately make their findings known to all interested parties from the Air Ministry down to theSquadron Commander, at which time the matter would be closed but the details would remain in the archival records of the Air Ministry until they were needed or eventually disposed of after a suitable period of time, which could be twenty years.

Boards of Inquiry were the official way in all military services, to dispose of problems which were of a personal nature and at times very touchy to the particular individual or individuals involved, as it was a way in which a collective decision could be made thereby exempting any one member of the Board from shouldering the burden, thus precluding any extraneous condemnation of the outcome being pointed at any one person. It was perhaps a way to dispel the sleepless nights of those who would find difficulty in reaching a fair and just decision by personal deductive logical processes.

The Fighter Command Armament Officer had arrived on the Station to carry out a thorough inspection of the ejection seat, which was fitted in Jeremy Gourd's aircraft. Messy as it was, with the blood and gore, which remained clinging to the metal parts, the officer carried out his task with unerring fortitude and completed the task in one day.

The reason why the ejection seat would be scrutinized so intently was the fact that it would ascertain whether or not the dead pilot had activated the firing handles, of which there were two, and to establish the correct function of the mechanism, should the firing system be activated. Futile as the inspection was, it must of necessity, be completed to the acceptance of the Board of Inquiry and for the peace of mind of the deceased pilot's family. In the final analysis it was not much satisfaction to anyone concerned, knowing that Jeremy Gould did not activate the firing handles and given all the factors, knowing that such an action was impossible due to the height the aircraft was from the ground when the accident occurred and the split seconds it took to impact the ground, the thinking and response time to the situation precluded any remedial action.

The next day, a practice of the aerobatics program would be carried out, this would be the first flying since the accident, which was only two days ago, but it would be good to get back to normal operations and proceed with the future plan of honing the aerial maneuvers which would be an integral part of the upcoming Air Show.

Thursday morning was slightly overcast and promised to clear later in the day so the flying program was delayed for a few hours but the hours of daylight practices were limited and it was a policy to fly at the precise time the flying would be carried out on the day of the show, which started promptly at three in the afternoon to fit in with other scheduled aerial displays.

Noon passed and all aircraft were ready for flight and Gaunt instructed the pilots to inspect their individual aircraft and check all systems which could be operated on the ground. Briefing was scheduled for two o'clock and the weather forecast was promising so all participants began thinking about the next two or three hours, keying themselves for the flying which would be approached with some trepidation and most certainly with meticulous care and precision.

Briefing was short and very concise and Gaunt tried to keep the atmosphere light and friendly joking with particular individuals in the hope that all in attendance would feel the mood and lift their spirits for the coming aerobatics.

At two thirty all aircraft were started and five minutes later all were taxiing to the active runway ready for take off. The weather was fairly good and acceptable for the flying about to be performed, it was however, decided, by Richard Gaunt that the afternoon's practice would take place over the sea which was only a few minutes flying time from the airfield and further more the height at which the final loop would be performed would be one thousand feet higher than normal. This was a precaution, which was not well accepted by the pilots, but all understood the safety factor involved in the reason for the decision made by the Squadron Commander.

The take off and climb to altitude was without incident and once into the aerobatics formation the aerial circus commenced at a command from Richard Gaunt.

It took thirty minutes to complete the full regime of the aerobatics program, which included very tight precision flying by three groups of seven in turn. The whole repertoire encompassed the full spectrum of aerial maneuvers, including loops, hesitation rolls, fast climbing turns and numerous formation changes, all of which was the prelude for the finale, culminating in the spectacle of the twenty one aircraft loop.

At the moment of truth, Gaunt called for the final arrowhead formation, which were formed at two thousand feet and once set, the command to execute the loop was given. As the formation gathered speed to the optimum, where they would pull up into the climb, the voice of Richard Gaunt could be heard clear and concise, as he called the movements from his position at the point of the arrowhead.

Any observer would have been in awe as this gathering of men and machines combined as one and completed the act by performing the most graceful of loops, maintaining a perfect symmetrical pattern as the arc was joined at the intersection of the initial climb.

The outcome of the Court of Inquiry into the tragic accident and the death of Flying Officer Gould was inconclusive, as the physical evidence of the remains of the fighter was beyond any form of reconstruction, which might have given some clues as to any mechanical malfunction, hence a superficial finding could not impugn the actions of the pilot nor positively identify a failure of any mechanical or electrical system of the aircraft. All that could be ascertained, was the fact that an unidentified situation caused the loss of human life and destruction of a fighter aircraft whilst a controlled aerobatics maneuver was in progress.

After the subsequent successful practice the remainder of the practices and dress went without a glitch and the finale at the Royal Event was a perfect display of aerobatic excellence and commended by all in attendance, culminating in a Royal Citation for the Black Eagle Squadron, which adorned the Squadron Commander's office and remains part of the historical archives of the meritorious actions of the Royal Air Force Squadron.

In the annuls of aerobatic flying, the display by the Black Eagle Squadron at that historic event has never been equaled and in all conscious logic, has never again been attempted, perhaps due to the irrevocable fact, that human life is too precious to flirt with.